# Designing and Reporting Experiments

# Open Guides to Psychology

Series Editor: Judith Greene, Professor of Psychology
at the Open University

# Designing and Reporting Experiments

Peter Harris

Open University Press
Milton Keynes · Philadelphia

Open University Press
Celtic Court
22 Ballmoor
Buckingham MK18 1XW
*and*
1900 Frost Road, Suite 101
Bristol, PA 19007, USA

First Published 1986
Reprinted 1988, 1989, 1991, 1992, 1993, 1994

**British Library Cataloguing in Publication Data**

Harris, Peter
  Designing and reporting experiments.
  (Open guides to psychology)
  1. Report writing
  I. Title
  808'.066      HF5719
  ISBN 0-335-15334-8

**Library of Congress Cataloging in Publication Data**

Harris, Peter
  Designing and reporting experiments.
  (Open guides to psychology)
  Includes index.
  1. Psychology – Experiments. 2. Psychometrics.
3. Report writing.   I. Title.   II. Series: Open guides
to psychology series.
BF200.H37 1986      150'.724      86-8621
ISBN 0-335-15334-8 (pbk.)

Typeset by Rowland Phototypesetting Limited,
Bury St Edmunds, Suffolk
Printed at Alden Press
Oxford and Northampton, Great Britain

*To Meriel for Antony and Richard*

# Contents

Contents

# Part 2:   Principles of Experimental Design

# Preface

Report writing is an important part of many courses in psychology, from 'A' Level to degree work. Despite its importance (in many cases marks for practical work and report writing contribute to the grade obtained for the course as a whole), there exists little published advice on how to go about writing reports. This guide is an attempt to alter this state of affairs.

It is a guide to *design* as well as report writing. Why? Because these elements are inextricably linked. You cannot write an effective report of an experiment unless you understand the whys and wherefores of its design. In order to fully understand what is required of you in the report, therefore, it helps to have an idea of the function that the report of a study serves in the scientific environment, which, in turn, requires you to understand something about the nature and purpose of empirical studies – especially experiments. But more than this, of course, many of the problems and difficulties you may face with report writing involve questions such as how to report the features of your design, or how to report adequately the outcomes of your *statistical analyses*. The answers to such problems depend on a knowledge of both the conventions of report writing and the logic and terminology of design. Consequently, this guide attempts to provide an introduction to both aspects of your practical work under the one 'roof'.


## How to use this guide

My aim as author of this guide has been to write something that will not only serve as an *introduction* to the problem, but that can also be used as a handy reference source throughout your career as a student of practical psychology. Consequently, I envisage the guide being used much like a thesaurus or dictionary – something that you turn to and read as the need arises. In particular, you may find yourself having to go over some of the sections a number of times before full understanding dawns. Don't be above doing this – it's what the guide is for. And, although you should never let yourself be *overawed* by the lab report, don't underestimate the task that confronts you either. Report writing is not easy – but I trust that this guide will make it easier.

Since this book is an Open Guide it is essential that you should take an active part in assimilating the text rather than being a passive receiver of information. After all, you are the only person who can diagnose what you already know and what you need to learn. This Guide will have been a complete failure if the information remains on the page rather than ending up in your own mind.

Where relevant, chapters begin with a number of 'diagnostic questions' with which you should test yourself to see whether you already have the required knowledge to tackle the chapter; if you have any difficulties answering these questions then you will be directed to another section of the Guide for assistance. In each part of the book you will find Self-Assessment Questions (SAQs) inserted in various points in the text. Attempting these SAQs will give you feedback on your learning and a better general understanding, and will help you be more of an active participant than a passive reader. The answers to these questions are to be found at the end of the book.

The summaries at the end of each section recapitulate the main points and so provide a useful aid to revision. The Index of Concepts that appears at the end of the book indicates the place in the text where each concept is introduced and defined, and entries in the index are in bold print in the text. It is also worth noting here that, for the special purposes of this Guide, all but one of my 'quotations' and 'references' have been dreamt up by me – they do not actually exist outside the covers of this book. The only exception to this is the extract in Section 2.2 from Eysenck, M. W. (1984) *A Handbook of Cognitive Psychology* published by Lawrence Erlbaum.

The guide is, of course, simply that – a guide. It is not a Bible. Indeed, such are the complexities of report writing and the inconsistencies between and even within departments in their reading of the requirements and conventions that surround it, that it would be impossible to write something that didn't confound somebody's beliefs and contradict somebody's practices. So, I'm sure that tutors will probably find that I have written something, somewhere with which they disagree. My only hope is that this doesn't induce fits of apoplexy and torrents of abuse. But my defence for what I have written is three-fold: firstly, the relative absence of existing and clear recommendations for report writing is a gap in our teaching that should be filled, and at least this is an honest attempt to fill it. Secondly, at the very least I hope this guide will act as a catalyst to the production of clearer and more widely accepted conventions. (For this reason I would welcome comment from students and staff concerning the things I have put here.) Finally, at all times my concern has been to relate the conventions I have outlined to the purpose the report serves in what I take to be its natural habitat – the research journal. This, I believe, gives us a yardstick against which to assess alternative recommendations.

Anyway, where there are important inconsistencies between the advice offered here and the practices followed by particular individuals, courses, or departments, I hope that tutors will make this clear to their students. So, students should watch out for this. And, of course, it should by now be clear that I do not intend the guide to *replace* adequate supervision – merely to *supplement* it.

Finally, although I have written this guide with students of *Psychology* in mind, I should imagine that many of the rules and conventions are shared by allied disciplines – such as Biology – and so it may prove useful to students of these subjects too.

### Statistics and the guide

Although the guide will deal with a number of aspects of analysis and design, we won't be able to deal with the mechanics of statistical tests themselves. Similarly, we will only cover the really basic statistical issues here. For a more comprehensive coverage of statistics, therefore, you will still need to refer to your statistics textbook. One that complements the coverage provided by this guide is 'Learning to Use Statistical Tests in Psychology: a Student's Guide' by Judith Greene & Manuela D'Oliviera, published by the Open University Press. Where relevant I will refer to this as 'GandD'.

I would like to take this opportunity to thank the many friends, teachers, colleagues, and students who have put up with me over the years, especially those who helped me during the writing of this book. In particular, I wish to express my gratitude to those in the Department of Psychology at Nottingham University, for giving me a home for the last five years, and especially for stinging me into action.

Chris Blunsdon and Dave Dingwall provided vital computing advice and support, Mel, Dibs, Janet, and Anne (among others), important friendship. My parents, brother, and Mer, were, of course, always there when needed, as were Antony Owen and Richard Gareth (though sometimes when not!). As usual, Sarah was tolerant, good-humoured, and supportive, where most of us would not have been. To all of these, and others unmentioned, many thanks are due and, I trust, hereby delivered.

Finally, I have long intended to acknowledge my debt to Mr Gareth Evans. He taught me Biology at school and, without realizing it, by his infectious enthusiasm started the whole thing off.

# Part 1:
# Writing Experimental
# Reports

# 1   Some Preliminaries

When you first signed up for a psychology course, the chances are that you didn't really expect what was coming, particularly the emphasis on methodology and statistics. For a few of you this may have come as a pleasant surprise. For most, however, it will undoubtedly have been a shock to the system.

I have here neither the room nor the inclination to justify academic psychology's scientific aspirations. My task is simply to help you as best I can to face up to one of the major educational consequences of this – the prominence given in most psychology courses to practical work (especially *experiments*) and the requirement in most instances to write up at least some of this work in the form of a highly structured and disciplined *practical report*.

All a report really is, is the place in which you tell the story of your study – what you did, why you did it, what you found out in the process, etc. But in doing this you are more like an ancient storyteller, whose stories were structured in accordance with widely recognized and long-established conventions, than a modern novelist who is free to dictate form as well as content. Moreover, like the storytellers of old, although you will invariably be telling your story to someone who knows quite a bit about it already, you are expected to present it as if it had never been heard before, spelling out the details and assuming little knowledge of the area on the part of your audience.

The nature of your story – the things you have to talk about – is revealed in Figure 1.1.

1. What you did
2. Why you did it
3. How you did it
4. What you found (including details of how the data were analysed)
5. What you think it shows

**Figure 1.1**   Information to be provided in the practical report

Our first clue as to the nature of the conventions governing the report comes with a glance at its basic structure. The report is in *sections*, and these sections (by and large) follow an established *sequence*. What this means is that, in the telling, your story is to be cut up into chunks: different parts of the story are to appear in different places in the report. The typical sequence of the sections appears in Figure 1.2.

Title
ABSTRACT
INTRODUCTION
METHOD
RESULTS
DISCUSSION
REFERENCES
APPENDICES (if any)

**Figure 1.2**   The sections of the practical report

The exact relationship between the elements of your story and the sections of the report is shown in Figure 1.3.

INTRODUCTION      What you did
                  Why you did it
METHOD            How you did it
RESULTS           What you found (including details of how the data
                  were analysed)
DISCUSSION        What you think it shows

**Figure 1.3**   Where the information in Figure 1.1 should appear in the report

The METHOD is composed of a number of sub-sections (Figure 1.4). Unfortunately, there is some disagreement over the precise order in which these sub-sections should appear. Although in this guide I will use the order illustrated in Figure 1.4, you may be advised to employ a different one. This is fine: the important thing is that you report the appropriate material in the right way in these sub-sections.

METHOD
                  DESIGN
                  SUBJECTS
                  APPARATUS and/or MATERIALS
                  PROCEDURE

**Figure 1.4**   The sub-sections of the METHOD

The report, therefore, is a *formal* document composed of a series of sections in which specific information is expected to appear. We will discuss the precise conventions governing each section as we go along. There are, however, certain *general* rules that we can introduce you to straightaway.

The first of these concerns the person to whom you should address your report, whom I shall call your **reader**. A very common mistake, especially early on, is to assume that your reader is the person who will be marking the report. In reality, however, this person will be marking your report *on behalf* of someone else – an idealized, hypothetical, person who is *intelligent*, but *unknowledgeable* about your study and the area of psychology in which it took place. Your marker will, therefore, be checking to see that you have written your report with this sort of reader in mind – that you have *introduced* the reader to the area of psychology relevant to your study, provided him/her with the background necessary to understand what you did and why you did it, spelt out and developed your arguments clearly, defined technical terms, and provided precise details of the way in which you went about raising and analysing the data you obtained. In short, therefore, you should write for someone who is *psychologically naive*, taking little for granted about your reader's knowledge of things psychological. So, when in doubt, *spell it out*!

On a much less fundamental level, you should separate the sections from each other by putting their titles (e.g. Design, Results, Discussion) as headings in the text. (The only exceptions to this are the TITLE, and in some cases, the INTRODUCTION.)

*SAQ 1*
In which sections of the report are you expected to give an account of (a) what you *found* in your experiment? (b) what you think your findings have to tell us?

*SAQ 2*
'The person who marks your report is a professional psychologist. As s/he knows quite a bit about the subject already, you can safely assume that s/he will understand what you did and why you did it without this having to be spelt out by you in the report. You should, therefore, direct your report at the expert, specialized reader.' True, or false?

## 1.1 *Experienced students, inexperienced students, and the report*

The demands and expectations placed upon you will of course vary with your experience of report writing. Early on in your career as an author of practical reports less will be expected of you than later, especially in what are really the key sections of the report – the INTRODUCTION and DISCUSSION. At this early stage you will be expected principally to show that you understood what you did in your practical and its implications, together with evidence that you have at least a basic grasp of the demands of the report's format.

In particular, little will be expected of you here in the 'why you did it' part of the INTRODUCTION (Figure 1.3). There are a number of reasons for this, but the main one is that the early studies you do in your practical course tend not to be justifiable in the terms we use here – that is in *research* terms. Generally speaking, these early practicals are chosen for you and, more often than not, are chosen for reasons other than their earth-shattering research significance. It would be rather perverse of us, therefore, to expect you to fabricate some plausible research justification for undertaking such studies.

Later on, however, (as you begin to take more responsibility for the design of your study) you will be expected to pay more attention to the research significance of what you did. This *why* part will then become more important – because, in being responsible for the choice of topic and design, you will be expected to be able to *justify* this choice – that is, to tell us *why* out of all the options available to you, you decided upon the study you conducted. And these will need to be *research* justifications, not merely ones of expediency! You will need, therefore, to develop the habit of thinking about how the ideas you are entertaining for your experiment or study will look in the report, paying particular attention to how they will fit into the INTRODUCTION. Specific dangers you must watch out for here are, firstly a lack of adequate material (*references*) to put in this section and, secondly, the undertaking of a project that lacks any research justification (because it is based on assumptions that are contradicted by existing findings in the area).

*Summary of Section 1.1*

1. The practical report is composed of a series of separate sections in which specific information is to be reported. Your task in the report is to tell your reader all about the study you conducted.
2. You must write, however, for an imaginary person – someone who knows nothing about your study or the area of psychology in which it took place.
3. This means that you should spell out the precise details of your study and provide your reader with a knowledge of the background relevant to it (previous findings in the area) when writing the report.
4. The demands placed upon you with regard to this task will vary with your experience as a student of practical psychology. In particular, as you progress you will need to get into the habit of thinking about how the ideas you are entertaining for your experiment or study will fit into the report, paying particular attention to how you will be able to develop and defend your arguments in the INTRODUCTION.

## 1.2 Writing the report

Before running your study you should really have a good idea of exactly how you are going to do it, as well as why it's worth doing, and how it relates to previous work in the area. However, you will have no real idea of what you are going to find and, therefore, no precise knowledge of the implications of your study. Thus the INTRODUCTION and METHOD could, in principle, have been written before you conducted the experiment, because these sections report material that you should have decided upon in advance. The RESULTS and DISCUSSION, however, could not have been written in advance, as these depend critically upon the outcome of your study.

However, although the order in which the sections appear basically reflects this historical sequence (Figure 1.2), it is ill advised to *write* them in this order. For some of the sections – such as the INTRODUCTION and DISCUSSION – require greater thought and effort to complete adequately than others. Consequently, you would be wise to work on these sections when you are at your freshest, leaving the more straightforward ones – such as those that comprise the METHOD – to those moments in which your interest in what you are doing is at its lowest ebb. In particular, never leave the DISCUSSION until last. I have seen too many reports in which students have devoted the better part of their time to the earlier sections, and lost interest in what they were doing by the time they reached the DISCUSSION. The consequence is a perfunctory DISCUSSION, and a poorer mark than they would have obtained had they budgeted their time more sensibly. Always bear in mind that the DISCUSSION is the key section of the report; it is there that the true value of what you have done in your study will be revealed in all its glory, when you come to assess the *implications* of your findings. How much have our findings added to the stock of knowledge that we described in the INTRODUCTION? In a very real sense, the whole experimental process – from design through to the writing of all the other sections of the report – is intended to clear the ground for the DISCUSSION – so write your report with this in mind. (Again, this will become more and more important as you begin to play a larger role in designing your own studies.)

Finally, the ABSTRACT is invariably better left until last, even though it is the first section to appear in the report. (Indeed, it is difficult to imagine writing an abstract of an unfinished report.) A good idea, therefore, is to write the ABSTRACT on a separate piece of paper and to attach it, together with the TITLE, to the front of the finished report.

*SAQ 3*
Which sections of the report could, in principle, have been written *before* you conducted the experiment? Why?

*SAQ 4*
Which is the key section of the report?


## 1.3 Writing style

Most of the features of the writing style adopted by psychologists stem from the scientific aspirations of the discipline. Thus the aim of the style is to give an objective, impersonal, trans-historical, appearance to work in the area. It is for this reason that critics of these scientific aspirations have doubted the propriety of these conventions (for they argue that psychology cannot be objective, impersonal, and trans-historical). At the same time, it can be criticized for the impetus it gives to the production of some quite excruciatingly tortured and pretentious prose. Nevertheless, it is the style still adopted and encouraged by most teachers of psychology, so here are its main features.

The first feature is perhaps the one to have suffered most from the recent attacks on the impersonal style of psychological writing. This is the requirement to write in the passive form – that is, to use constructions such as 'an experiment was conducted' and 'it was found that' rather than 'I conducted an experiment' and 'we found that'. Previously, the use of the first person (I, Me, My etc.), was the preserve of the Illustrious. Nowadays, however, it appears more frequently in journal articles, and I have begun to find myself reluctant to correct it in students' reports (time was, I would have covered them in red ink and scorn). Nevertheless, because it is a somewhat harder style to adopt, and because it is still the generally accepted one, the passive form will be employed in the examples provided in this guide. At the very least this will give you something on which to model your reports.

The second feature is *definitely not* open to disregard. This is the requirement, central to the construction of your INTRODUCTION, to *substantiate all factual assertions*. A **factual assertion** is simply anything that could prompt your reader to ask 'who says?'. Anything that could be re-written as 'it was *found* that' or 'it was *argued* that' or 'it was *claimed* that' etc., can be regarded as a factual assertion and requires substantiation. You are expected to tell the reader at least by *whom* it was found (argued, or claimed) and *when*. So, if you make a firm statement about *any* aspect of the psychological universe (however trivial), you must attempt to support it.

In practice, this means that statements such as: 'There is no difference between the sexes in the detrimental effect of emotion on ability to reason logically' or 'It has been found that the arousal of anxiety enhances the impact of a persuasive message' are not allowed. However, statements such as: 'There is no difference between the sexes in the detrimental effect of emotion on ability to reason logically (Outram, 1969, 1972; Northwood and Bidlake, 1972a; Freshwater, Smith, and Gibson, 1976)' and 'It has been found that the arousal of anxiety enhances the impact of a persuasive message (Brooke, 1984)' are perfectly permissible. The reason being that the latter contain what we call **references**, whereas the former do not.

The use of references is the preferred method of substantiating factual assertions in psychology, for they provide direct answers to the questions *who* and *when*. So, wherever possible you should cite a reference (at least a name and date) for all *quotations*, definitions, and *findings* at all times, even where you have made the citation before. You must make it clear to which author, and to which particular piece of his or her work, you are referring at *any given time*. For example:

> Asbury (1984) found that although the induction of emotion adversely affected the ability of her subjects to reason logically, it did not affect her female subjects any more than her male ones. Indeed, she found this to be true irrespective of whether the emotional arousal was positively or negatively valenced (Asbury, 1984). On the basis of these data she argued that 'the traditional viewpoint that the reasoning abilities of women are disrupted by the arousal of emotion, whereas those of men remain unaffected, is simply untenable' (Asbury, 1984, pp12–13).

Where there is more than one author, or you are referring to several publications by the same author(s), you should bear in mind some additional points. Firstly, with more than one author, for the initial mention of a piece of research, you must cite *all* their names (e.g. Hellawell, Hayward, and Valentine, 1981). In all subsequent citations of this particular publication you may then cite the reference using the first author's name only, with the Latin *'et al.,'* denoting that there are additional authors (e.g. Hellawell *et al.*, 1981). Where there are only two authors, however, you should cite *both* names at all times.

With multiple publications by the same author, you should cite these *chronologically* (e.g. Bostock, 1974, 1982, 1983, 1985). Where the same authors have published more than one relevant piece of work in any given year, suffix the year with a letter (e.g. Jones and Wills, 1979a). Make sure that you use the same suffixes in the remainder of the report and also in the REFERENCES *section*. For quotations, definitions, etc., you should also cite the appropriate page number *in the text* (not in the REFERENCES section), as in the example above.

Finally, where you wish to use a number of references to substantiate the same factual assertion (which is quite commonly) then put these in *chronological* order, starting with the earliest reference and working through to the most recent one. However, don't split up an author's work here: put *all* relevant work of any given author in the place obtained by his or her *earliest* piece of work. Where the earliest work of different authors comes in the same year, put these in *alphabetical* order. At all times separate the reference to different authors by semi-colons. The finished product should look something like this:

> Much mental energy has been expended on the question of the relationship between attitudes and behaviour (Bostock, 1974, 1982, 1983, 1985; Jones and Wills, 1979a; Hellawell *et al.*, 1981; Howarth, 1981b).

And, while I'm on the subject, please ensure (a) that the reference exists (b) that it says what you claim it says and (c) that you have referenced it correctly. And never invent references!

Where there are no references to substantiate your assertions, then the next best thing is to think up some examples that are consistent with your viewpoint. This should apply more often to 'A' Level students and others who lack access to a university or college library, than to undergraduates. Nevertheless, I suppose it is feasible (just!) that later on in your career as an undergraduate you may find yourself working on a study that is *so* novel that you can find no previous relevant work. But make sure that the problem arises because of novelty – not because you have failed to do the preparatory reading expected of you.

If you haven't been given the references to read for your practical, and if you have access to a university or college library, then one way of finding relevant material is to thumb through recent editions of the more reputable journals, looking for an article on the topic, preferably with plenty of references and with a good summary of work in the area. There are also abstracting services available (such as *Psychological Abstracts*) that you might use. If even after this you are really stuck for references, or if you lack access to such sources, then you have no option but to dream up examples that substantiate your viewpoint. But the important thing is precisely this: *that you should attempt to substantiate your viewpoint.* In psychology you should *never* find yourself having made a claim about an aspect of the psychological universe without attempting in some way to shore it up. And this is particularly true of what you will come to know as your *experimental hypothesis.* You should always attempt to justify these – especially as you become more experienced.

*SAQ 5*
If you make a statement that might prompt your reader to ask 'who says?', what should you do?

*SAQ 6*
Correct the following references:

> Abel, Baker, and Cartwright (1985) found that performance on the experimental task improved considerably in the presence of a group of peers. This contradicted previous findings in the area (Dawkins and Edgar, 1977,1977: French, 1962,1983: Garbage, Henchman and Janitor, 1984). As Abel, Baker, and Cartwright put it '. . . it is not clear why this happened'.

Above all else, you must learn to develop your arguments logically, and to articulate them clearly. One aspect of this will involve you in *defining* terms. When in doubt, always define the critical terms you are employing in your report – at least this way we know whether we all understand the same thing by them. And use a *professional* **definition** whenever possible – often, as psychologists, we use the same term (e.g. attitudes, perception, emotion) in a way that has different connotations from the way a layperson might use this term. You can obtain professional definitions from other work in the area, text-books etc., and there are also available dictionaries of psychological terms. Also, if you wish to use **abbreviations**, make sure you define these on their first appearance – by writing the term to be abbreviated out fully, together with the abbreviation in brackets (e.g. 'the Galvanic Skin Response (G.S.R.)'; '. . . this is known as an Independent Variable (I.V.)'). After this you can simply use the abbreviated form.

You may also find that you need to include **illustrations** and tables in your report. These are generally desirable as they enhance the presentation of your work, and aid your reader's comprehension. Where you use these you should observe the following rules:

1. Label all figures, tables, graphs, and **diagrams** (for which the term 'figure' may be used) consecutively, starting with the first one of each class to appear (e.g. Figure 1, Figure 2, Figure 3, Table 1, etc.,).

2. Use these labels when referring to them in the text (e.g. 'The precise layout of the equipment is shown in Figure 1').
3. Give them all informative titles, and label tables and graphs clearly.

You will find plenty of examples of such useage in this guide.

A final part of the style is a comparatively recent development, and one that has perhaps yet to meet with universal acceptance. This has to do with **sexism**. Formerly, it appeared that all subjects and all experimenters were male – these individuals were referred to with the masculine form of the third person (he, him, his etc.). Sometimes this was ludicrous – as when experimenters who ran studies with only female subjects still referred to them using this convention. (I've even read something on the psychological effects of being pregnant that used it.) Nowadays, with greater awareness of the sexist implication of conventions such as these, you would be extremely unlikely to have anything accepted for publication that contained such useage. So, moral considerations aside, the habit of non-sexist writing is probably worth acquiring from the outset. As a general rule, therefore, only use 'he' or 'she' when you are actually referring to a male or female. Otherwise use alternatives (there are plenty of examples of how to do this in this book, some clumsy, some less so).

*Summary of Sections 1.2–1.3*

1. The DISCUSSION is the key section of the report. It is there that the true value of your study will be revealed, for it is there that you come to assess the implications of your findings. You should therefore budget your time when writing the report so that you devote sufficient thought and attention to this section.
2. When writing the report you will be expected to adopt a particular style of writing. The critical features of this style include the need to substantiate all factual assertions (preferably by using *references*), and to develop and articulate your arguments clearly and logically.

*1.4  The report as a research instrument*

So far, therefore, we have introduced you to the basic requirements of the report, and given you some idea of how to go about writing it. One thing we have not done, however, is said anything about *why* the report takes the form it does: why is it in sections? why do these sections come in a particular order? why are there restrictions over what material is to be mentioned, where it is to come, and how it is to be expressed? These are good questions. The answers to them require us to understand something of the function of the report in its **research** context.

Those of you who have already written reports may well have found yourselves confused and frustrated at some stage or other by rules of format and principles of construction that strike you as being rigid, restrictive, inhibiting, and more or less arbitrary. One of the main reasons for this is that you meet the report in a strange environment. For the report is primarily a *research* instrument. Its natural habitat is the academic journal. The rules and conventions that govern its construction have evolved for the purpose it serves there. In its educational setting, therefore (where you meet it) these conventions are often difficult to comprehend, because you have inherited the report divorced – at least at first – from its principal function.

In its research context, the report serves to inform those who may be interested in a researcher's work of its *nature*, *purpose*, and *implications*, in as *clear*, *thorough*, and *concise*, a way as possible (note the conflicting demands). To this end, the idea of a general format, with clearly labelled sections in which clearly defined pieces of information are to be provided, has been developed (Figure 1.5). In theory, using this format it should be possible for a would-be reader to establish *quickly* whether the reported work is of interest, to *locate* any particular piece of information s/he wants and, if s/he so desires, to even *re-run* the study (to conduct what we call a *'replication'*) with the minimum of effort and, in most cases, *without recourse to any other document*.

The conventions that govern the construction of the report, therefore, have been developed for the purpose of conveying information clearly, precisely, quickly, and concisely, to those who are interested. And these are the same conventions that you must obey in report writing, even though very few of you are ever likely to have your work read by fellow researchers. In essence, these conventions have been *transplanted* from the research world into the educational one.

INTRODUCTION:   1.  Summarize state of area prior to study. (Why you did it)
2.  Sketch study in broad outline. (What you did)
3.  State your *experimental hypothesis* (or hypotheses) (section 8.4)

| METHOD: | 4. Outline precise details of study. (How you did it) |
| RESULTS: | 5. Present relevant data, together with outcomes of appropriate statistical analyses. (What you found) |
| DISCUSSION: | 6. Summarize and interpret findings. |
| | 7. Assess implications for area (i.e. return to 1.). (What you think it shows) |

**Figure 1.5**   The requirements of the research report.

*SAQ 7*
What principal purposes are served by the conventions of the *research* report?

As you progress, you will be expected more and more to emulate the research process – to design your studies with their research implications in mind, and to write your reports with greater emphasis on the implications of what you have done for existing findings and ideas. As a result, more will be expected of you in the report, particularly in the INTRODUCTION and DISCUSSION. So, those of you who will be expected to progress in this way must watch out for this transition, which will probably occur for most of you when you enter the second year of an undergraduate course.

As this is critical to the way in which you should write your report (and as it will obviously affect the way your report is marked) if you have any doubts about which group you fall into, then ask your tutor. Indeed, this is a general rule for anything in this guide: when, in doubt, ask your tutor.

*Summary of Section 1.4*

1. The practical report is related to the research report. The conventions that govern the construction of the research report have been developed for the purposes of conveying information clearly, precisely, quickly, and concisely to those who may be interested in a researcher's work.

2. To a large extent, these are the same conventions that you must obey when writing your practical reports, particularly as you become more experienced (e.g. as you move into the second year of an undergraduate course in psychology).

# 2   The Introduction Section

*Diagnostic questions on design for Chapter 2*

1. What is a *variable*?
2. Which variable do we *manipulate* in an experiment?
3. What is the name of the variable that we *measure* in an experiment to assess the effects of our manipulation?
4. Which hypothesis predicts that there will be a *difference* between conditions in an experiment? Is it (a) the Experimental Hypothesis or (b) the Null Hypothesis?
5. What is a *confounding* variable?
6. How do we generally *control* for confounding variables in an experiment?

If you have difficulties answering any of these questions, turn to Chapter 8.

The first major section of the report then is the INTRODUCTION. As its name implies, the purpose of this section is to *introduce* something. Which raises two questions, both of which you should be able to answer on the basis of your reading of Chapter 1.

*SAQ 8*
So, in the INTRODUCTION, you introduce *what*, to *whom*?

Essentially in the INTRODUCTION to your report you should fulfill the following requirements, *in the following order*:

1. Review the background material (existing findings and theoretical ideas) relevant to your study.
2. Outline the precise problem you chose to investigate and describe the way you went about investigating it.
3. Outline the results predicted by your **experimental hypothesis** (section 8.4).

This means that your INTRODUCTION is effectively in *two* parts: a part in which you deal with work that pre-dated your study (which will generally be the work of *other* people), and a part in which you finally introduce and discuss briefly your *own* study. You must move, therefore, from the *general* to the *specific*. That is, you do not start with a description of your study – you build up to it. Why you do it this way should become clearer as we go along.

As the INTRODUCTION is logically in two parts, we shall deal with them separately here. So, let's now turn to the first part of your INTRODUCTION, the part in which you review the background material relevant to the study you conducted.

## 2.1  The first part of the INTRODUCTION: Reviewing the background to your study

First, a word of caution. If you have read around your subject, there is a great temptation, whatever your level as a student, to let your marker know this by hook or by crook. Most frequently this is achieved by weaving every little morsel into the INTRODUCTION, regardless of how contrived this becomes. *Resist this temptation*, for it is counter-productive. The material you mention should be *directly* relevant to the problem under investigation. Moreover, you should avoid the more trivial details of the studies you report, emphasizing instead their major findings and conclusions. For your task in this part of the report is primarily to put your study into its research context, by showing its relationship to previous work in the area. Consequently, material should be mentioned *only if it is relevant*. So, if you end up having read something that turns out to be rather tangential, drop it from the report, however much heartbreak this causes you.

At the same time, however, always bear in mind that you are under no obligation to treat published work as 'gospel'. From the outset you are as entitled to disagree with the viewpoints of others as they are with you. It is the *manner* in which you do this that is important. Don't be afraid to disagree with what someone has argued if you believe you have reasonable grounds for doing so, but make sure that you can provide plausible support for your viewpoint. That is, *you must seek to substantiate your point of view vis à vis* theirs.

## 2.2  Inexperienced students, experienced students, and the Introduction

If you are taking your first course in psychology, or an 'A' level in the subject, or you are simply in the first year of a degree course, you will probably be considered a novice. At this stage in your career as psychologists (and for many of you this may well be as far as you need to go), you are basically learning your trade. Consequently, your marker will generally be looking to see whether you've understood the study you conducted, and whether you have a grasp of at least the basic demands of the practical report format; basically, whether you're putting the right material in the right sections.

For you, then, the more important part of your INTRODUCTION will actually be the second part – where you talk about your study. The first part of your INTRODUCTION will really only be a general sort of orienting section – one which gives your reader some idea of the area in which your practical took place. In order to do this you will generally need to include accounts of one or two of those studies most directly relevant to the one you conducted. But you probably won't be expected at this stage to spend much time attempting to *derive* your study from the work that went before it.

It's difficult to give general advice here because studies vary so much, as do markers' expectations. But if you're completely bewildered, one general strategy that you might employ runs as follows:

1. Identify the particular aspect of the discipline in which the practical took place – e.g. Cognitive psychology; Social psychology. Start with a brief statement about the nature of this area and, if meaningful, a definition of it.
2. Introduce the aspect of this larger area to which the study was relevant – e.g. memory, attention, attitudes, rumour etc.
3. Then talk about the particular aspect of this topic that your study specifically addressed – e.g. the impact of mnemonic devices; the 'cocktail party' phenomenon; attitude measurement; how rumours are spread.
4. Then, with the problem nicely set up, you are ready to introduce your own study to your reader.

This has been done in outline in the example below:

Cognitive Psychology is concerned with 'attempts to identify the processes and mechanisms that underlie human cognition' (Eysenck, 1984, pxiii). One such process or mechanism is the Human Memory. (Provide definition.) One aspect of our ability to recall that is of great practical as well as theoretical interest is the possibility that we might be able to improve it. In this regard a number of techniques for improving memory have been developed – known collectively as 'mnemonic devices'.

One such technique is known as the *method of loci*. (Describe technique.) But does it work? For instance, although Korman (1897) reported distinct improvements in his subjects' ability to recall a list of everyday objects when using this technique, a recent attempt to replicate his findings (Johnson, Donohoe, and Vitkovitch, 1985) was unsuccessful.

Notice that what you are doing here is effectively 'honing in' on your study. Rather than dropping your reader in cold by starting with your study, you're taking it step-by-step and easing him/her in gently. Now, it may not be possible to do it quite so neatly each time, but you should always *try* to lead up to your study. This is a good rule: don't *start* with the details of your study; build up to them.

*SAQ 9*
Why is it a good idea to build up to the details of your study, rather than starting the INTRODUCTION with a description of what you did?

Starting with such an approach from the outset will result in you developing good habits for later when – at least for those of you who must progress – more will be expected from you in the first section of the report. For, as you become more experienced – for instance, as you move into the second year of your undergraduate course – this first part of your INTRODUCTION will become longer. It will also take on some of the functions that the INTRODUCTION has in a research paper. For now you should be beginning to undertake studies that have at least some limited research justifications. Or at least you must write them *as if* they had research justifications.

In the INTRODUCTION to a research report, the author will summarize the state of the area *prior* to the study s/he conducted. Subsequently, s/he will re-address this material in the light of the study's findings, to see whether the position has changed at all (i.e. whether the study itself has allowed us to make much progress). S/he does this in the DISCUSSION. Essentially, therefore, the report spans two separate time periods – the time immediately *before* the study was undertaken (reported in the INTRODUCTION), and the time immediately *after* the study had been completed and the resulting data analyzed (dealt with in the DISCUSSION). The report therefore embodies progress because we essentially re-visit the area, looking at the problems and issues addressed in the INTRODUCTION with the benefit of any new knowledge gleaned from the study's findings. It's all a bit like one of those 'before and after' ads in which the advertiser is at pains to illustrate the contrast between circumstances prior to, and after, the use of his or her product. The INTRODUCTION is the equivalent of a *before* picture. The DISCUSSION is the equivalent of an *after* picture. You can see this process built into the sections of the research report summarized in Figure 1.5.

It is now time for the INTRODUCTIONs you write to ape this function. Thus, at this stage in your career, you should be attempting in the first part of your INTRODUCTION to show how the omissions in previous work – be it flaws in the studies conducted, or simply questions and issues that have yet to be addressed – form the basis of the study you undertook. For it is your task to expose here the advance you propose to make – the gap in our knowledge that your study is designed to plug. At this stage, therefore, you should be starting not only to give a rather more detailed account of the previous work of relevance to your study, but you should also be looking to *derive* your study from this work (i.e. to show how your own study builds out of previous ones).

*SAQ 10*
How does the research report, in principle, 'embody progress'?

This requirement has obvious implications for how you should conduct yourself at the *design* stage of your studies. Essentially, it will be ill advised to dream up and run your studies without first doing your background reading and thinking about how you will go about *justifying* your study in your INTRODUCTION. Remember that studies tend to evolve from the time at which you first start to think about research questions that interest you, to the time at which you start to run your first serious subject. And thinking about how your study fits into the existing literature is a critical part of this process. In particular, you should never find yourself having undertaken a study that flies in the face of existing *findings* without having sound arguments for doing so. For you will, of course, need to be able to articulate these arguments in your INTRODUCTION.

What this means in practice is that you must *do your preparatory reading*. And you must design your study *in the light of what you find there*! Do not jump straight into your study, or you will run the risk of conducting something for which there is no theoretical justification and which, therefore, is going to be exceedingly difficult, if not impossible, to write up. Always bear in mind that your practical work does not begin and end with the study itself – it ends with the completion of the *report* of that study. You will, therefore, have to be able to give an account of what you did that shows this to have been justified.

*Summary of Sections 2.1–2.2*

1. The purpose of the INTRODUCTION is to put your study into its research context, by providing your reader with an introduction to the background material (existing findings and theoretical ideas) relevant to it.
2. This material is presented in the first part of the INTRODUCTION. The second part of the INTRODUCTION presents the reader with a brief introduction to your study.

3. Increasing emphasis is placed on the first part as you become more experienced and the reports that you write begin to emulate research reports.

### 2.3   *Your own study*

In the second part of your INTRODUCTION you turn – *for the first time* – to your own study. Here at last you are free to move away from talking about other peoples' work and are able to introduce your own. But note that the emphasis is firmly on *introducing* your study. You will not be expected at this stage to give a detailed account of what you did; there will be room enough elsewhere in the report for that. Here all that is required is a paragraph or two succinctly outlining the following features of your study:

1. Briefly state the problem you chose to investigate.
   This should, of course, be clear from what you have written in the INTRODUCTION so far. But it is good policy to confirm the problem. Then neither you, nor your reader, should be confused over the issue you tackled.
2. Give your reader a *general* idea of how you went about tackling it.
   There are usually a number of different ways you could go about designing experiments to test the same proposition, so here you need to make some general reference to the way you actually chose to do it.
3. State clearly and accurately your *experimental hypothesis* (or hypotheses) and clarify why your experiment tests these.

Please note that this is directed at all of you. Although we made exceptions in the first part of the INTRODUCTION for those students we classed as 'inexperienced', *all* of you – regardless of level – will be expected to include the above material in the final part of your INTRODUCTION.

Now, don't be put off by this – it all sounds much more complicated than it is. You can, in fact, generally achieve this in one or two short paragraphs, and to give you some idea of how you might go about it, below you will find an illustration of the sort of approach you can adopt. This is an extract from the introduction to an experiment which examined how varying the imageability of the words a subject had to memorize (i.e. how easy it is to construct mental images of the concepts denoted by these words) affected the usefulness of a mnemonic device (an aid to memory). The three features outlined above are all contained in the final paragraph of this extract: the problem is alluded to in the first sentence, the second sentence indicates the principal change to the previous study, and the final sentence states the experimental hypothesis.

> . . . Unlike Richards (1984), however, Johnson *et al.* (1985) failed to find any effect of the nature of the material upon the ability of their subjects to memorize lists of words using a mnemonic device (in this case, the *method of loci*). However, as they did not allow their subjects any time to become accustomed to the mnemonic device, it may well be that their findings simply illustrate the need to be practised in the use of these devices before any significant improvements in memory performance can be revealed.

> Consequently, a replication of Johnson *et al.* (1985) was undertaken. In this instance, however, provision was made for those in the mnemonic condition to become proficient in the use of the device prior to the start of the experiment proper. If, as Korman (1897) suggested, the *method of loci* depends for its success upon the imageability of the material employed, we should expect those subjects using the device to recall a greater number of words from the easily-imaged list, than from the hard-to-image list, as well as more words from the easy-to-image list than are recalled from this list by those not using the mnemonic. If, however, imageability is not important, we should expect no such difference.

Note that although we have talked about the INTRODUCTION being in two parts, this is *not* indicated in the format of the section itself. That is, you *do not* separate the part in which you introduce your own study from the earlier part of the INTRODUCTION by things such as a separate title or by missing a line. Simply start a new paragraph.

No doubt some of you are still rather confused by all this. If so, don't worry – remember that good report writing is a skill. Consequently, it invariably takes time to develop. You should not be surprised, therefore, if at times you find yourself uncertain and confused about what is required of you. Just do your best to develop this skill by practising it – by writing reports and getting feedback on your efforts from your tutor. And, if you're really stuck, look for examples of how other people have solved the problems that confront you. So, if you have access to a university or college library, look up some journal articles and see how their introductions have been ended.

At the beginning of this section it was stated that the most important thing was for you to make a clear and accurate statement of your **experimental hypothesis**. Here's how you go about this:

1. State the experimental hypothesis clearly – mention in this statement both the Independent and the Dependent variables. Say, for example, 'It was predicted that those who consumed the standard quantity of cheese three hours before going to bed would report a higher incidence of nightmares than those who did not consume cheese during this time', rather than 'It was predicted that cheese would affect nightmares'.

2. Note, however, that you do not at this stage refer to these explicitly as the Independent and Dependent variables. Nor will you need at this stage to state whether your experimental hypothesis was bi-directional or uni-directional. You will find that this material is to be put in the DESIGN. It is there that you will make a formal statement of the features of your design. Thus, in this part of the INTRODUCTION you will not need to include the material in brackets below:

> The experimental hypothesis (was bi-directional and) predicted a difference in the incidence of nightmares (the dependent variable) as a function of manipulating the subjects' intake of cheese three hours before they went to bed (the independent variable).

3. This goes for the null hypothesis as well. You will not need to state here what the null hypothesis is in your experiment because, to all intents and purposes, the null hypothesis is the same for all experiments. You can assume, therefore, that your reader knows what a null hypothesis is, and is aware that you have one. At this stage of the report you only need mention what your predictions were under the theories discussed in your INTRODUCTION. (Although you must assume that your reader is naive psychologically, you can take it for granted that s/he has at least a basic grasp of the fundamentals of experimental and statistical logic.)

Now your experimental hypotheses should bear a meaningful relationship with the issues you addressed in the first part of your INTRODUCTION. That is, they should be linked to what has gone before. So don't, for example, suddenly spring upon your reader a set of experimental hypotheses that *contradict* the ideas that have been addressed in the first part of your INTRODUCTION. If you wish to disagree with existing arguments or findings in the literature then include also arguments (ideally substantiated by *references*) in the first part of your INTRODUCTION outlining and *justifying* your own viewpoint. Similarly, don't set up hypotheses that bear no relation to what has gone before – remember that your INTRODUC-

TION is designed to set the scene for your experiment, and therefore principally functions to show how you arrived at your hypotheses. Similarly, never confuse the experimental and null hypotheses. Finally, you must not mention the *results* of the experiment in this section.

*SAQ 11*
Why not?

*SAQ 12*
What purpose does the INTRODUCTION serve?

*Summary of Section 2.3*

1. The second part of the INTRODUCTION should outline the purpose of your own experiment.
2. After confirming the specific problem you investigated, you need to clarify the way in which your experiment tackles this problem.
3. Finally you should state clearly your experimental hypothesis.

# 3   The Method Section

*Diagnostic questions on design for Chapter 3*

1. What is a *within* subjects design?
2. What is a *between* subjects design?
3. What are the principal advantages of a *within* subjects design?
4. What are the principal advantages of a *between* subjects design?
5. What is a *mixed* design?

If you have difficulties answering any of these questions, turn to Chapter 9.

The next section in your report is the METHOD. This section is composed of a number of sub-sections. In these you talk about various aspects of the study you conducted. The sub-sections are:

| | |
|---|---|
| *Design –* | in which you talk about the formal design features of the experiment you ran, using the appropriate terminology (things like the independent variable, dependent variable, and experimental hypothesis). |
| *Subjects –* | in which you describe the relevant features of the people who participated in your experiment as *subjects* (i.e. the people from whom you obtained scores on your dependent variable). |
| *Apparatus &/or Materials –* | in which you describe the equipment &/or less bulky materials you used. |
| *Procedure –* | in which you give a blow-by-blow account of precisely what you said and did to your subjects in the experiment. |

The METHOD, in the form of its various sub-sections, is designed to give the reader a coherent, clear and precise account of what you did in your experiment – who your subjects were, what you told them about the experiment, how you presented your materials to them, in what sequence you did things etc. In fact, this section is rather like a recipe in a recipe book: the first three sections (DESIGN, SUBJECTS, and APPARATUS &/or MATERIALS) correspond to the *ingredients* part; the final section (PROCEDURE), to the part in which you are told what to do with them.

The watchword of this particular section is *thoroughness*. Your aim should be to provide all the information necessary (and in the right sections) for your reader to be able to repeat *precisely* what you did for his/her self – to undertake what we call an **exact replication** of your study.

Why? Well, not only might other researchers disagree with the inferences we eventually draw from our experiment – i.e. the conclusions we reach – but they might also dispute the actual *findings* we obtained. They could argue that the findings on which we based our conclusions were anomalous and that if the experiment were run again (i.e. were *replicated*) they would obtain different results. For this reason we have to present the details of our experiment in such a way that anybody who thought this – that is, anyone who doubted the **reliability** of our findings – could test this possibility for themselves.

This is an important argument. Findings that are not *reliable* – that are markedly different each time we conduct the same experiment – have no place in the construction of a science. The whole logic of experimental design – of manipulating one variable and looking for the effects of this on another (in order to determine cause–effect relationships) – relies on these relationships remaining constant. It is no good if the causal variables appear to change – that on Monday, for instance, smoking causes lung cancer, but by Thursday it doesn't. To construct an adequate science of psychology, we have to be able to build on our findings. We must be able to take certain findings as read (as 'facts') after experimental evidence has accumulated and use these as *assumptions* in the subsequent research and theorizing we do.

In other parts of your course you will find that people are increasingly questioning whether this is actually achievable in psychology. But that is not our province in this book. Here we are only concerned to give you the skills necessary to see for yourself whether experiments work. Moreover, there are those who argue that more straight replicating work should be undertaken in Psychology, in order to discover how reliable our findings are. And this is another good reason why you *must* be clear and thorough in the various sub-sections that make up the METHOD.

*SAQ 13*
What is an *exact replication* of a study?

*Summary of Section*

1. The METHOD is composed of a set of sub-sections: DESIGN, SUBJECTS, APPARATUS &/or MATERIALS, and PROC-EDURE.
2. It is designed to give a clear and accurate statement of what you did in your experiment, so that other people will be able to *replicate* it if they so desire.

## 3.1 The design section

There are a variety of ways of going about experimenting in Psychology – ways of ordering conditions, using subjects, controlling for potentially confounding variables – and your experiment will involve you in having to choose one particular way of putting your ideas into practice. The method you choose is known as the *design* of your particular experiment. The process by which you come to choose it is called *designing* experiments.

The DESIGN itself is generally one of the briefer sections of the report. All you need to give here is a brief but formal statement of the principal features of the design you employed. In particular, you will need to state:

1. What type of design you used (i.e. whether your experiment had a between, within, mixed, or a matched-subjects design).
2. What your Independent Variable (IV) was, including details of the conditions you selected to represent different levels of the IV. You must do this for all the independent variables in your experiment.
3. What your Dependent Variable (DV) was, including details of the units in which subjects' scores were measured. You must do this for all the dependent variables in your experiment.
4. What the experimental hypothesis was – but you don't need to state the null hypothesis.

*SAQ 14*
Why is there no need to state formally the null hypothesis of your experiment?

This must be a *formal* statement of the design; that is, you must use the terminology that has been developed over the years to enable us to talk accurately about features of experiments – things like the IV, DV, and experimental hypothesis.

However, although students generally get the format of this section right, they sometimes get confused over things like what their IV or DV was, or whether they used a *between* or a *within* subjects design. So make sure that you understand these concepts, for you will be expected to write a proper DESIGN regardless of whether or not you played a part in designing the experiment yourself. (And this will apply to the remainder of the METHOD as well – that is, to the SUBJECTS, APPARATUS &/or MATERIALS, and PROCEDURE.)

Again, as with the description of your study at the end of the INTRODUCTION, this can be done comparatively simply. Indeed, the DESIGN really amplifies and clarifies this earlier statement of the purpose of the experiment. Below is an example of how this can be done:

### DESIGN

The experiment had a mixed design. The independent variables were: (1) whether the words were drawn from an easily-imaged list or from a hard-to-image list (within subjects); and (2) whether the subjects received or did not receive instruction and training in the use of the *method of loci* mnemonic (between subjects). The dependent variable was the number of words of each type correctly recalled by the subject after ten minutes delay. (Mis-spellings were counted as errors.) It was predicted that those employing the mnemonic would recall more words from the easily-imaged list than from the hard-to-image list, and more easy-to-image words than those *not* employing the mnemonic.

*SAQ 15*
What purpose does the DESIGN serve?

## *Summary of Section 3.1*

1. The DESIGN section is a brief section in which you make a clear and accurate statement of the principal features of your design.
2. It is a *formal* statement and consists of a precise description of the design you employed, what your IV and DV's were, and what the experimental hypothesis was.

## 3.2 The subjects section

The second part of your METHOD is the SUBJECTS. Here you are expected to give a brief description of the critical features of the **subjects** who participated in your study – that is, those from whom you obtained the data you analysed. But don't mention any other participants here – for example, experimental stooges (or *confederates*) who actually took part in the experiment as actors – or people who helped you code questionnaires, videotapes etc. Simply restrict yourself to a description of those who were *subjected* to your manipulation of the IV and contributed the scores you analysed.

There are two aspects of the subjects of your study that are of interest to us: who they were, and how they were distributed.

Who your subjects were is of importance because this contributes to the *generalizability* of your findings. That is, to the extent to which we can extrapolate your findings to other groups of human beings (section 5.5). For example, are they relevant to everybody, regardless of race, class, gender, age? Or are they circumscribed in some way – for example, relevant only to middle-class, white, youthful Britons, of above average intelligence?

Many studies in psychology, for example, use undergraduate psychology students as subjects. Yet students, of course, tend to come from a restricted sector of the population. They are invariably young, supposedly intelligent, and predominantly middle-class. Add to this the probability that those interested in psychology may also have peculiarities of their own, and it could be that the findings of studies based on samples of undergraduate psychologists can be extrapolated only to the subset of the population from which they come.

However, the validity of this criticism depends on the IV being investigated. If the variables which *differentiate* such subjects from the general public (e.g. age, intelligence, class) are thought to have some impact on the Dependent Variable (e.g. reasoning, attitudes) then the criticism may be valid. But other variables may not be so influenced (e.g. motor skills, visual perception). So, don't *automatically* assume that having a student sample seriously limits the extent to which you can generalize your findings. And always bear in mind that – if your study is in other respects well-designed – the results should be generalizable to at least some sub-group in the population. After all, in some respects at least, students are still members of the human race. And, believe it or not, there are young, middle-class, intelligent people who are not students.

The other issue – how your subjects were distributed among your experimental groups – is at this stage rather more pressing. We would want there to be no systematic differences between the subjects in your groups, other than those introduced by your manipulation of the Independent Variable. That is, we don't want more of those who were better at the experimental task to appear in one particular condition.

*SAQ 16*
Why not?

For this reason, therefore, it is sometimes a good idea to present a breakdown of your subjects by condition. For then your reader can satisfy him/her self that this was the case.

As a general rule, therefore, you should describe your subjects in terms of those variables that are likely to have an influence on the Dependent Variable. In practice, however, most of you, most of the time will need only to describe your subjects in terms of the characteristics generally reported in this section: sex, age, and occupation.

So, your subjects section should ideally read something like this:

1. Mention the number of subjects per condition, including a breakdown of the sexes.
   But please avoid here the 'mixed-sex' joke. That is, saying that the subjects were of 'mixed-sex'.
   It'll only prompt your tutor to make some kind of idiotic remark in a strenuous effort to be funny.
2. Mention the age *range*, together with *mean* or *mode*, of the

overall sample (breakdown by condition only if there's a lot of variation between the groups).
3. Give us some idea of the overall range of occupations.
4. State the means of selection (e.g. randomly, in response to a questionnaire etc.).
   And don't lie about this!

This can in fact be done quite simply:

### SUBJECTS

Twenty subjects took part in this experiment, ten per condition. Twelve subjects were female, six of whom appeared in the mnemonic condition. The subjects varied in age from 18 to 28, with a mean of 19.8 years. All subjects were undergraduates at the University of Nottingham, although none were students of psychology (the majority – 15 – were reading for degrees in engineering and science). Subjects were recruited personally by the experimenters in the refreshment areas of the Portland Building. None of them were acquaintances of the experimenters.

*SAQ 17*
What information does your reader require about the subjects in your study? Why?

If you do a class experiment in which you split up into groups and take it in turns to be experimenter and subject, beware here. In all probability your experiment will be based on the whole class – in which case you should treat the *class* as a whole as your subjects here, rather than reporting the bit of the experiment you carried out yourself. If in doubt, check this with your tutor.

Do not include *procedural* details here (Section 3.4).

*Summary of Section 3.2*

1. In the SUBJECTS section you provide a brief description of the critical features of the individuals who provided you with the data of your study.
2. The purpose of this account is to tell your reader *who* your subjects were and *how* they were distributed across your experimental conditions, so that s/he can assess both the *generalizability* of your findings and the possibility that there were any *confounding variables* arising from the composition of your experimental groups.

## 3.3   The apparatus and/or materials section

Unlike many other sciences, studies in psychology vary a great deal in the amount of equipment used. At one extreme, we might simply use a pen and paper. At the other, we might find ourselves using expensive equipment to monitor subjects' performances in specially equipped rooms with on-line control of stimulus presentation and data collection. But, be it hi-tech or ever-so-humble, the place to describe the equipment used in your study is here.

The first thing to decide is whether you used **materials** or **apparatus** – for this will dictate the title you give this section. Unfortunately, the difference between them is pretty vague: essentially things like pencils and paper, playing cards etc., come under the rubric of materials, whereas bulkier items – such as tachistoscopes, video-cameras, cassette-recorders etc., would be called apparatus. However, *do* try to decide which of these types of equipment you employed in your study, and label this section accordingly. You should only label the section 'Apparatus and Materials' if you are sure that you used *both* types of equipment.

One problem you may face here is what to do about a questionnaire or scale you employed in your study. Some tentative advice on what to do under these circumstances can be found in Appendix 2.

If you only used materials, then this section will probably be little more than a description of the items you used. But make sure that you write this in coherent sentences. It must not just be a *list* of the items. Write as below:

### Apparatus and Materials

The words were presented randomly by an Acorn BBC Microcomputer on a monitor mounted immediately in front of the subject. They consisted of 25 single words that were comparatively easy to image (e.g. garage, desk), and 25 single words that were comparatively difficult to image (e.g. conscience, love). These were matched across conditions for length and frequency, and were presented singly, centre-screen, for a duration of 5 seconds, with a 5 second interval between items. All items were obtained from the lists published by Johnson *et al.* (1984) (see Appendix 1 for a full list of the items used). Subjects recorded their responses on a piece of paper.

Note that this section has been labelled 'Apparatus and Materials' because a microcomputer and monitor qualify as *apparatus*, response sheets, pens etc., as *materials*.

Where you use apparatus, there is a little more scope for expansion in this section, especially if the layout of the equipment is either complex or theoretically important. Under these circumstances, don't hesitate to draw a good, clear diagram of the layout (section 1.3), and describe the apparatus *precisely*. You would need, for instance, to mention not only that a cassette-recorder was used, but to state precisely what *make* and *model* of cassette-recorder it was.

*SAQ 18*
What is wrong with the following section?
    *Apparatus*
    Microcomputer
    Cassette-recorder and microphone
    Playing Cards
    Response buttons
    Video Camera
    Pens and Paper

Perhaps the commonest mistake made here in this easiest of sections, is to describe the *function* of the equipment – the *use* to which it was put. Strictly speaking, such detail is *procedural*, and therefore belongs in the PROCEDURE. So, do not describe *how* the equipment (material or apparatus) was used here. Simply outline *what* was used and, if relevant, how it was linked together. That is, the section should really only describe the basic *nature* and *layout* of the equipment used.

*Summary of Section 3.3*

1. In the APPARATUS and/or MATERIALS section you describe the equipment used in your experiment.
2. You should describe this thoroughly, accurately, and clearly, using diagrams where these might clarify the picture.

### 3.4 The procedure section

The final part of your METHOD is the PROCEDURE. In many respects, this is one of the most difficult of the report's sections, because it requires the learning of a rather subtle distinction between procedure and other aspects of methodology. Perhaps the commonest mistake is to include here material that should have appeared at the end of the INTRODUCTION. For in the PROCEDURE we do not concern ourselves with the broad strategy of our experiment. We are simply interested in a narrow aspect of the campaign – what *precisely* happened to our subject from the moment we started running him/her, to the moment we finished. This section should provide a blow-by-blow account of more or less everything we said and did to a typical subject, in the order in which we did it.

Imagine that instead of being asked to give an account of an experiment in a report, we are in fact writing about an episode of a soap-opera that we produced. In order to produce this episode, we have to operate at a number of levels. The episode has to fit into the story-line that has been developed before. We hope we've established this in the INTRODUCTION, which is effectively a brief synopsis of the story so far (the existing research) for those who've missed previous episodes (the psychologically naive reader). We need a set of equipment to record the episode and props, scenery, and locations, to provide the background to the action, or even to play a role in the events that take place. This we've described in the APPARATUS and/or MATERIALS section. Similarly, we need a list of the key characters who participate in the episode – those not involved on the experimenter's side of the fence have been described in the SUBJECTS section. So far, therefore, so good. All this material provides the necessary *background* to our own episode. However, we have yet to talk in anything other than the barest detail about the actual *events* that are to take place: the key interactions between the characters, the critical props, and the crucial pieces of dialogue. That is, we have yet to give our readers any idea of how, in practice, we realized the action first mentioned in the latter part of the INTRODUCTION, and summarized in the DESIGN. It is the equivalent of this sort of material – the key points of the script – that should appear in the PROCEDURE.

In principle, you should be aiming to tell your reader everything s/he needs to know in order to *replicate* your study exactly. So, *precision* and *thoroughness* are the watchwords of this section. Everything of relevance in your procedure should be mentioned in this section, therefore – it can be pedantic to the point of being tortuous. However, there are techniques that enable you to lessen the burden on your reader. For instance, you usually need only describe the procedure in detail for one of your subjects. With this done, you can generally outline where the procedure in the other conditions varied in fundamental respects from the one outlined. (There should be enough commonality between the procedures in your different conditions to enable you to do this – see below). This, of course, is where our analogy with an episode of a soap-opera transparently breaks down. If anything, in an experiment you have a number of distinctive versions of the script to report – versions that are identical in all respects other than those involving your manipulation of the Independent Variable.

Why should these different versions of the script be identical in all respects other than those involving your manipulation of the Independent Variable?

Where you have lengthy instructions, you can usually record the gist of them in this section and refer to an *appendix* in which the full text of the instructions is given. But you should always report any *critical* features of your instructions (e.g. where the instructions manipulated the IV) **verbatim** here – that is, where this happens you should report *exactly* what you said, together with what you said differently to different subjects.

Errors that frequently occur in this section are, firstly, failing to state clearly whether your subjects were run individually or in groups, and, secondly, describing how the data was scored and rendered for analysis. The PROCEDURE should end with the completion of the subject's input to the study (including follow-ups, where these have been employed), not with an account of what you as experimenter did with the scores you'd obtained (that belongs at the start of your RESULTS).

### Procedure

Subjects were run individually in a sound-proofed experimental cubicle. From the outset they sat facing the monitor on which the words were to appear, with the experimenter sat immediately behind them, to the subject's left and out of his/her sight. The subject was informed that the experiment involved an examination of 'our ability to recall lists of items'. The equipment and its function was described to them, they were informed of the experimental procedure, and any outstanding questions were dealt with. (See Appendix 2 for full instructions. These were read by the experimenter.)

Once the experimenter had satisfied himself that the subject was aware of what was required, and that all outstanding questions had been dealt with, the experimental session began in earnest.

Those in the mnemonic condition were given instruction in the use of the *method of loci* (see below). They were told to imagine a familiar room and to practise placing in various parts of this room mental images of items in a list of words presented to them. These were presented to them singly, on the monitor, for a duration of 5 seconds with an inter-item interval of the same duration. There were 2 sets of 10 practice items, with no item appearing more than once. Subjects recalled immediately after the presentation of the final stimulus in both lists.

At this stage, those in the no-mnemonic condition were simply asked to 'practise recalling' the practice items. These were the same items, presented in the same manner as above. In all other respects the instructions given to the groups were identical.

Once the practice sessions were over, the subject was told that the experimental session proper was about to commence. Subsequently, the experimental items were presented to them.

Once the items had been displayed, the subjects were prevented from recalling for 10 minutes. During this interval the subjects were given sheets containing simple addition and subtraction tasks to perform. At the end of the ten minutes they were asked to recall as many of the items as they could, using the pen and paper provided. When the subject was satisfied that s/he had recalled as many items as s/he could, the experiment was brought to a close, and the subject de-briefed. In particular, attempts were made to discover whether those in the no-mnemonic condition had employed mnemonics on their own initiative (particularly ones that might be based on the use of mental imagery) and whether those in the mnemonic condition actually used the recommended technique during the experimental session.

### 3.5  Instructing and running subjects

As you can see, one of the most critical features of your experiment is the **Instructions** you give to your subjects – what you tell them about your study, how you tell them what to do, etc. Consequently, an account of your Instructions is a central feature of your PROCEDURE.

In the first place your Instructions should be the *only* verbal communication that takes place between you and your subject during the experimental session. Secondly, in some studies you may actually find yourself *manipulating* your independent variable via the instructions you give to subjects in the different conditions. And even where you are not using your instructions to manipulate your independent variable, you may still often need to give slightly different instructions to those in the different conditions. At all times, however, it is important to make your instructions as *similar* as you can *between* conditions, and *identical* within conditions.

*SAQ 20*
Why?

For reasons such as these, therefore, you should always attempt to *standardize* the instructions you give. That is, you should look to make them as consistent as you can *between* conditions in *style, content,* and *delivery*, and there should be *no* variation in these elements in the same condition. Thus, if you choose to read your instructions to your subject, you must make sure that you do so in the same manner, and with the same inflections, throughout – you must, in effect, become an actor delivering his or her lines. If you doubt your ability to do this, then it may be a good idea to record the instructions on tape and to play this tape to your subjects instead. Equally, you might type them out and simply give them to your subjects to read themselves.

Writing good instructions is, in fact, a highly developed skill. It is one that you will acquire as you go along. They should be friendly, couched in terms that your subject will understand, and containing enough material for your subjects to be able to perform the task you give them adequately, but often without at this stage giving too much away. For this reason it is important to give your subject an opportunity to ask questions *prior* to the start of the experiment. But restrict yourself to answering questions about the task that confronts them, rather than addressing the wider aims of the experiment – there should be time set aside to discuss those at the end. And make sure that you do all this *before* you start the experiment in earnest. Satisfy yourself that the subject understands what is expected of him/her before you commence – we don't want interruptions, as this will destroy the control that you have built so carefully into the design of your experiment.

Once you have started to **run** your subject, you should attempt to keep uncontrolled contact to a minimum. Thus you should avoid unscripted vocal contact, as well as any form of non-verbal contact such as head nodding or shaking that might influence your subject's performance. At this stage you should be *friendly*, but *uninformative*. Of course this will make for a rather bizarre and artificial encounter – but that's the name of this particular game. And it may not be easy. Not surprisingly, your subject may well attempt to subvert the order you have imposed by making remarks about his/her performance that invite your comment. You must resist this and remain non-committal if you wish to remain loyal to your experiment. But it may be worth thinking about the extent to which this feature of experimenting in psychology may influence the sort of data we obtain. It is another aspect of experimental psychology that has come under criticism.

As well as instructions and demeanour, you should be prepared for your subject in other respects too. Once s/he is with you, you should be able to devote the greater part of your attention to actually *running* him/her. Subjects are valuable! So, you should prepare everything you can *in advance* – e.g. things like response sheets, random sequences of orders, etc., so that you are free to attend to your

49

subject. And don't forget to acquire the information you will need to compile your SUBJECTS section (gender, age, occupation, and any other information that may be relevant to your particular study (e.g. right or left handedness, quality of eyesight, ability to read English etc.).

*Summary of Sections 3.4–3.5*

1. In the PROCEDURE you give a blow-by-blow account of everything that was said and done to a typical subject in your experiment, so that those who wish are able to replicate it *exactly*.
2. Make sure that you *standardize* your instructions, so that they are identical within a condition and as similar as possible in style, content and delivery *between* the different conditions in your experiment.

# 4   The Results Section

**Diagnostic questions on statistics for Chapter 4**

1. What are *inferential* statistics?
2. What is a *significant* difference?
3. What does it mean to say that the 'five per cent significance level' was used in an experiment?
4. Distinguish between the *obtained* value and the *critical* value of a statistic. How do these function in the process of *hypothesis testing*?

If you have difficulties answering any of these questions, turn to Chapter 10.

Of all the sections of the report, the RESULTS is probably the one that is most frequently mishandled by students. Yet it is really one of the most straightforward of the report's sections. All you need to do in this section is to report the *findings* of the study in the most appropriate manner, resisting in the process any temptation to *interpret* them as you go along. That is, a bit like a journalist of the old-school, you must distinguish rigidly between 'fact' and 'comment'. In this section you must not go beyond any statement of what the findings actually *are* ('fact'), to a statement of what they appear to you to *indicate* ('comment').

In theory, what constitutes the **findings** of your study depends on the *nature* of that study. In practice, however, most of you, most of the time, will be reporting the results of *experiments*. In experiments you invariably generate numerical or **quantitative** data (that is, data in the form of numbers) in order to test hypotheses. This means that there will be *two* aspects to your findings, *both* of which you should report here. Firstly, you must give an account of the *data* you obtained. Secondly, you must give an account of the nature and outcomes of whatever *inferential* statistical analyses you performed on these data.

## 4.1  Describing the data

If you reported *all* the data from your experiment – all the numbers you gathered – it would be quite difficult for your reader to interpret what the scores of your subjects had to tell us. For very few people are capable of grasping the essential message of a set of data from looking at the **raw scores** (the actual numbers obtained from the subjects themselves). We therefore need a way of conveniently and simply summarizing the main features of a set of data. **Descriptive statistics** provide a way of doing this. These are statistics that *summarize* the central properties of a set of data. They enable us to assess, almost at a glance, things like whether or not the scores of our subjects tend to be similar to each other or whether they vary quite a bit (measures of **variation**), what score best typifies the data as a whole, or the performance of subjects in one particular condition (measures of **central tendency**), etc. Answers to questions like this enable us to work out what *inferential* questions are worth asking of our data.

For instance, imagine that we ran an experiment and obtained the data in Table 4.1. In this form it is difficult to make much sense of these data. It is not easy to tell much about the comparative performance of the subjects in the two groups. The scores appear to vary quite a bit from individual to individual, but is the *overall* performance of the subjects in the two groups all that different?

**Table 4.1** Raw Scores (mean for each subject) from an experiment with one control and one experimental condition.

| Experimental Condition | Control Condition |
|---|---|
| 17.3 | 6.8 |
| 39.2 | 14.1 |
| 20.7 | 61.2 |
| 79.3 | 61.7 |
| 42.7 | 94.8 |
| 56.5 | 49.7 |
| 24.9 | 37.2 |
| 57.9 | 23.9 |

In Table 4.2 the same data are expressed in terms of a few *descriptive statistics* (the **mean**, which tells us what score describes the performance of an archetypal member of each group, and the **standard deviation**, which tells us something about the extent to which the scores vary from individual to individual within each group). We are also told the number of subjects in each group.

**Table 4.2** The same data as in Table 4.1 expressed in terms of three descriptive statistics.

| | Experimental Condition | Control Condition | Usual notation for these descriptive statistics |
|---|---|---|---|
| MEAN | 42.3 | 43.7 | $\bar{X}$ |
| STANDARD DEVIATION | 20.01 | 27.3 | S |
| NUMBER OF SUBJECTS IN EACH CONDITION | 8 | 8 | n |

Now our task is much easier. From Table 4.2 we can see, perhaps to our surprise, that the typical performance in the two groups is not all that much different, especially given the extent to which the scores of the subjects within the two groups appear to vary (the standard deviations in the two groups are quite high given the mean scores). Looking at this table it would be surprising indeed (and in the event we would probably want to check our calculations) if we were to find a significant difference between our two groups.

Because of the difficulties inherent in grasping the essential features of *raw* data, therefore, we tend *not* to put raw data in the RESULTS. Instead, we present an account of its principal features (such as *central tendency* and *variation*) in the form of descriptive statistics. Such material we usually display in a suitably *labelled* and informatively *titled* **table** – such as Table 4.2. (If you wish to include the raw data, then you should put this in an appendix.)

Generally speaking, therefore, there should usually be at least *one* table in your RESULTS. However, sometimes it is still not possible to fully grasp the main features of a set of data from even its descriptive statistics. If you wish to enhance your reader's comprehension of the data, therefore, you might go one step further and present a **graph** of it – especially as many of those who go blank at the sight of numbers have little problem in grasping the message of a well designed graph.

Don't be afraid, therefore, to deploy the techniques at your disposal to facilitate your reader's (not to mention your own) comprehension of the basic features of your data. However, don't go overboard here – in an experiment, at least, this aspect of your findings is invariably less interesting than the outcomes of your *statistical analyses*.

*Summary of Section 4.1*

1. In the opening paragraph of the RESULTS reiterate briefly what data was gathered from your subjects (e.g. response time, number of items recalled – i.e. a statement of what your *dependent variable* was). This both sets the scene and ensures that the reader does not have to hunt through the METHOD to understand your results.
2. In general, you should not include the *raw* data in this section (i.e. the scores provided by each subject). Instead, you should provide a potted account of your data in the form of descriptive statistics such as group means, Ns and Standard Deviations. These should generally be presented in tables.
3. However, the use of tables *alone* is not sufficient; you must include also some explanatory text describing what data appears in the table, and the precise outcomes of any analyses relevant to it.
4. You might also consider the use of graphs or other methods of displaying your data visually if you think this will improve the reader's understanding of the data. Such methods, however, should be used *in addition* to tables, not *instead* of them.

## 4.2 Describing the outcomes of your inferential statistics

As well as *describing* the data, you will also need to report the nature
and outcomes of whatever *inferential* statistics you calculated from
them. You must report a number of features of these (see Table 4.3).
Firstly, you should make a *clear and accurate* statement of *precisely*
which test you employed. Secondly, you should report the precise
value you *obtained* for the statistic you used (i.e. the value you
*calculated*), together with whatever additional information is necessary in order to enable your reader to look up the relevant *tabled* or
*critical value* in the appropriate tables (things like d.f.'s, N's etc. –
Table 4.3). Finally, you need a statement of whether or not the value
you obtained was significant. If it was significant, you indicate this by
stating the level at which it reached significance (e.g. $p < 0.05$, or
$p < 0.01$). You can, in fact, report all this information surprisingly
succinctly: e.g. 'There was a significant effect of relatedness on time
taken to reach criterion ($t = 2.43$, df$= 5$, $p < 0.05$)' or 'There was no
effect of reinforced practice upon the time taken to reach criterion
($F1,32 = 1.25$, ns)'. What this means in practice is that you need not
put here the *workings* of the tests you undertake. If you wish to
include this material, then put it in an *appendix*.

**Table 4.3**  Characteristics of some common inferential statistics

| Test | Statistic | Information necessary to find critical value | Relationship of *obtained* to *critical* statistic for significance |
|------|-----------|----------------------------------------------|---------------------------------------------------------------------|
| Wilcoxon signed-ranks | W | Number of pairs of scores (N) | Equal to or less than the critical value |
| Mann-Whitney U test | U | Number of scores in the two groups (n1 and n2) | As above |
| Chi-square | $\chi^2$ | Degrees of freedom (df) | Equal to or greater than the critical value |
| t-test | t | Degrees of freedom (df) | As above |
| Analysis of Variance | F | Degrees of freedom (df1 and df2) | As above |

*Summary of Section 4.2*

1. Once you have introduced and described the data, you should describe the nature and outcomes of the inferential statistics you calculated from that data.
2. State precisely *how* the data was analysed – i.e. what *tests* were used. Describe the appropriate statistical test accurately, e.g. do not say that a 't-test' was used, but state which *type* of t-test, e.g. a 'related t-test', and whether it was a once or a two-tailed test. If you use analysis of variance remember to be precise in your description of the type you employed. You will need to state something like a 'two-way, between subjects' analysis of variance was used.
3. You need only mention the *type of test* used (accurately); the value of the *obtained statistic* (e.g. t=2.43); the *degrees of freedom* or whatever alternative is necessary for someone to look up the appropriate *critical* value (e.g. df=5, N=32); and whether or not this was *significant*. If it was significant, report at what level (e.g. p<0.05). If it was not significant, you need only state that it was 'not significant' (the convention 'ns' will usually suffice for this).
4. Make sure, however, that you distinguish between what you found – the numerical data and results of statistical analyses – and what you believe it to show – your inferences and conclusions. Include only the *former* in this section. The latter should appear in the DISCUSSION.

Here is an example of how a basic RESULTS section governed by these conventions might look.

*Results*

The number of subjects who reported having nightmares during the course of the experiment are shown in Table 4.4.

**Table 4.4** The number of subjects reporting nightmares in the cheese and no-cheese conditions.

|  | Cheese | No Cheese |
| --- | --- | --- |
| Number reporting nightmares | 33 | 22 |
| Number not reporting nightmares | 17 | 28 |

These data were analysed using Chi-Square. There was a significant association between the consumption of cheese and the incidence of nightmares ($\chi^2$=4.4, d.f.=1, p<0.05), with those consuming cheese three hours before going to bed reporting a higher incidence of nightmares than those not consuming cheese in this period.

If you have more than one set of data and attendant analyses to report, it will probably be more effective to construct *separate* tables for each set of data. In this case, consider the data *and* its attendant analyses as two sides of the same coin. So report them as a unit, by detailing the data first and then describing the outcomes of the analyses *before* moving on to the next data/analysis set. However, you should step through these in some kind of order of merit, starting with the data and analyses that are most fundamental to your experimental hypothesis and working through to the material that is illuminating but essentially ancillary to the main thrust of your argument.

This, then, is the material that you should present in the RE-SULTS. You should remember at all times that the principal aims here are ones of *clarity* and *accuracy* – you must give the reader a clear idea of the type of data you gathered, what its main features are, and the nature and outcomes of the inferential statistics you employed. Moreover, it should be clear at any given time *what* data you are talking about and *what* particular analysis belongs to that set of data, especially if you have used more than one DV and/or wish to test more than one experimental hypothesis. You should also make sure that you provide enough information in this section (e.g. in labelling the conditions) for the reader to be able to make sense of your data *without* having to turn to other parts of the report for clarification.

*SAQ 21*
Why should you provide the reader with such a clear idea of the type of data you gathered, its main features and the nature and outcomes of the inferential statistics you employed?

*SAQ 22*
If you were to come across the following statement in the RESULTS section of a research report, what criticisms would you have?
   The data were analysed using Analysis of Variance. The results were significant.

Finally, here are some general tips to help you avoid some of the commoner mistakes in this section:

1. Include enough information in this section for the reader to be able to make sense of your results without having to look elsewhere in the report. For example, take care to label conditions

or groups meaningfully in tables, graphs and text. Do not use meaningless or difficult-to-decipher abbreviations. If you do use abbreviations, include the key to these in this section as well.

2. Do not talk about the data *before* it has been analysed, i.e. do not 'eyeball' the data and discuss 'differences' if the data has yet to be analysed. Such numerical differences may fail to be statistically significant and the convention in psychology is to speak of differences only when these are significant. Otherwise, it is assumed that there is no 'real' or *reliable* difference. If you don't understand this, then turn to Chapter 10 and your text-book of statistics.

3. This also applies to any remarks you make *following* the analysis of the data. One of the commonest, and most damaging, failings is to talk of differences in the data, even though these have failed to achieve statistical significance. To do this is to confuse differences in *observed* sample values (which may have arisen through chance variation) with underlying differences in the *population* from which your samples are assumed to have been drawn. The purpose of *statistically* analysing your data is to assess the likelihood that the group values you have obtained in your study reflect important underlying differences in the population from which the samples were drawn. *It is the population differences that you are interested in!* So do *not* make this mistake! In the absence of the appropriate statistical analysis, we cannot tell whether observed differences in group values mean anything important or merely reflect the influence of chance variation. If you do not understand this, read Chapter 10 and your textbook of statistics. Now.

4. Abide by the **statistical decision** (i.e. whether to accept or reject the null hypothesis) you are compelled to make by your chosen statistical criterion (significance level). For instance, if your results fail to reach significance at the 5 per cent level then *accept* the null hypothesis and treat your data as you would any non-significant data. Although there is some dispute about this, in general this is the safest position to adopt. So, if you set up a criterion for significance, abide by it, *no matter how close to the magical significance level your results actually come.* Unless you actually *reach* this significance level, treat your data as non-significant. That is, if you hit the post, it isn't a goal.

5. You need not give the underlying details of statistical procedure (e.g. the rationale and workings of analysis of variance) or reasoning (e.g. the principles of hypothesis-testing) in this section.

One of the paradoxes of the practical report is that whilst you must assume your reader to be *psychologically* naive, you *may* assume that s/he has at least a rudimentary grasp of the basic principles of statistics and the rationale of hypothesis-testing.

6. Include sufficient information in this section to enable your reader to reach his or her *own* conclusions about the implications your data has. In principle, your reader should be capable of reasonably disagreeing with your interpretation of the data purely on the basis of the information you provide here.

7. Don't necessarily restrict yourself to reporting the obvious analyses – do not be afraid to squeeze all the relevant information from your data that you wish. But bear in mind that your aim is to communicate your findings, so avoid overloading this section with irrelevant and unnecessary analyses.

8. Include *all* the data in this section that you wish to comment upon in your discussion, however impressionistic, **qualitative** and unamenable to statistical analysis. The inclusion of descriptive data (e.g. a selection of comments from your subjects) is perfectly permissible, but should usually be used as a *supplement* to, rather than a *substitute* for, quantitative, numerical data.

Now in the abstract this all sounds rather complicated. So here is a further example of how you might go about writing a RESULTS section. If you have difficulty understanding any of the terminology in this, then don't hesitate to turn to Chapter 10 and your textbook of statistics for clarification.

*Results*

The number of words correctly recalled (excluding mis-spellings) from both the easy-to-image and the hard-to-image list were calculated for each subject. The mean scores for each condition are shown in Table 4.5.

**Table 4.5** Mean number of words correctly recalled from the easy-to-image and the hard-to-image list (n=10 for each group).

|  | Easy-to-image | Hard-to-image |
| --- | --- | --- |
| Mnemonic Group | 18.5 | 12.0 |
| No Mnemonic Group | 13.6 | 8.4 |

The data were analysed using a 2-way analysis of Variance for mixed designs. There was a significant main effect of condition ($F_{1,18}=28.2$, $p<0.001$) with those in the mnemonic group recalling more items overall than those in the no-mnemonic group. There was also a significant main effect of item-type ($F_{1,18}=93.3$, $p<0.001$) with more items from the easy-to-image list being recalled than from the hard-to-image list. However, the condition × item-type interaction did not reach significance ($F_{1,18}=1.2$, n.s.).

The majority of subjects (8) in the no-mnemonic condition claimed to have attempted to remember the items by 'rote-repetition', with the remainder employing simple attempts at organizing the material into semantically-related clusters. All those in the mnemonic condition reported using the *method of loci*, and most of these expressed their surprise at the impact this appeared to have had on their capacities to recall.

### 4.3  Rejecting the null hypothesis

Although rejecting the null hypothesis entails that we accept the **alternative hypothesis** that there is a genuine (statistically reliable) difference between our conditions, this does not necessarily mean that we can conclude that the *psychological* hypothesis underlying the experiment has been supported. After rejecting the null hypothesis we have, in fact, to *search* for the most reasonable explanation for our findings. This may well turn out to be the arguments we addressed in the INTRODUCTION (those that predicted the existence of a difference between these conditions in the first place) – but they needn't be. We can only decide this after a suitable discussion in which we consider and examine closely all the potential explanations for the findings we have obtained. And high on the list of explanations to be examined will be the question of whether the *control* that we exercised in the experiment was sufficient to enable us to make unequivocal inferences. This is why we require the next section – the DISCUSSION.

Moreover, what we have said here applies also to situations in which we have **accepted the null hypothesis**. Under these circumstances we also have to work out what this means *psychologically*, as opposed to statistically.

*Summary of Section 4.3*

1. Once we have decided whether to accept or reject the null hypothesis we begin the search for the most reasonable explanation of our findings.
2. In particular, we will need to assess the quality of the control that we have exercised in the design and execution of our study.
3. These issues are addressed in the DISCUSSION.

# 5   The Discussion Section

Researchers design experiments to test hypotheses to help solve practical problems or develop theories. However, in psychology at least, the outcomes of experiments are *not* self-evident. That is, they require *interpretation*. We need, in fact, to 'discover' what we've found out. For instance, in our cheese and nightmare experiment we may have been compelled by our data to *reject* the null hypothesis that there is no reliable difference between the experimental and control condition. Now, however, the real work begins. For we need to find out what *caused* the difference that we've found. Was it the independent variable (eating cheese)? Or are there *confounding* variables that could equally well account for this difference? The answers to such questions we can only arrive at by looking carefully at our experimental design and assessing the quality of the *control* that we exercised. Only once we've done this can we decide (for decision it is) which of the various options is the *likeliest* explanation for the findings we've obtained, and only once we've done this will we be able to begin to explore the *implications* of our findings for the area under consideration.

Moreover, this remains true of situations in which our data compels us *not* to reject the null hypothesis. Does this mean that the independent variable is *not* the causal variable we anticipated? Or was there some aspect of the design we employed that acted to *nullify* the impact that the independent variable would normally have on the dependent variable? Again, we can only decide this after a due examination of the design and procedure we employed. Again, we need to sort this out before we can even begin to assess the implications of our findings for the area we discussed in the INTRODUCTION.

The point is that our findings are subject to *uncertainty*. We need to interpret our results. This process is undertaken in the DISCUSSION.

There are three definable stages to this process of assessing our findings. These three stages, in sequence, provide the structure of the DISCUSSION. Firstly, we need to agree about what needs to be explained. So the first task in the DISCUSSION is to (1) state what the results of the experiment are by providing a précis (in words) of the RESULTS. Once this has been done, we need to try to *account for* these findings. Is the independent variable responsible for significant differences? If not, what is? Can we be sure that a set of non-significant results indicates the absence of a causal relationship between the independent variable and the dependent variable? The second task in the DISCUSSION, therefore, is to (2) explore these issues, arriving where possible at an assessment of the likeliest answer to them. Finally, you need to (3) explore the implications of your findings. For instance, if you've decided that on balance it seems likely that the independent variable was indeed responsible for the findings, what implications does this have for the material – especially the arguments and theories – you outlined in the INTRODUCTION? This, of course, is the key issue – the reason why we design and run research experiments in the first place.

We can crystallize these three phases of the DISCUSSION around three questions:

1. What are the findings of this study? (An outline of the results you've obtained.)
2. What do they mean? (What, if anything, do they tell us about the relationship between the independent and dependent variables?)
3. What are their implications? (With regard to the issues you outlined in your INTRODUCTION, together with some sort of consideration of the direction and form that *future research* should take.)

Of course the balance between these three phases, and the depth to which you will be expected to follow some of the issues raised by your findings, will depend on your experience as a student of practical psychology. As a novice considerably less will be expected of you here. Your main task will be to state your findings, examine what they mean, and outline and *assess* a few possible explanations of them. But you should try to do as well as you can. In particular, remember that you should be aiming to display clarity of thought and presentation when discussing the outcomes of your experiment.

Before we go through the phases themselves, two additional points need to be made. Firstly, if the findings of experiments are subject to uncertainty, you can imagine that the findings from techniques that provide us with even less control – such as correlations – are even more problematic. Secondly, with so much emphasis on assessment and interpretation, it is entirely possible that others will dispute our conclusions. Our task in this section, therefore, becomes one of arguing the best case we can from the data available to us.

## Summary of Section

1. The outcomes of psychology experiments are subject to uncertainty. They require interpretation in order to find out what they have to tell us about whether or not there is a causal relationship between the Independent Variable and the Dependent Variable.
2. The process of assessment and interpretation takes place in three phases in the DISCUSSION. These phases revolve around three questions: What are the findings of this study? What do they mean? What are their implications?

### 5.1 What are the findings of the study?

You should open your DISCUSSION by summarizing the main features of the RESULTS. Was there a significant difference between your conditions? If so, in what direction? Were the findings consistent with the experimental hypothesis? Doing this enables us to get clear from the outset what it is that has to be explained in the DISCUSSION. All of you, therefore, regardless of your level of experience, will need to do this adequately.

### 5.2 What do these findings mean?

Once we've decided what it is that we have to explain, we can set about attempting to explain it. If we have *rejected* the null hypothesis, then we need to find out how likely it is that this was brought about by our manipulation of the independent variable. Does it appear that it was eating cheese that was responsible for the differences between our experimental and control groups in the number of nightmares they reported? If we have *accepted* the null hypothesis, then how confidently can we conclude that this indicates the absence of a causal relationship between our independent and our dependent variables?

In order to answer these questions as well as we can, we need to examine our experiment for any features that might also have been responsible for the results we obtained. Essentially, therefore, we need to assess the quality of the *control* that we exercised in our experiment.

*SAQ 23*
Why should we be interested in the control we exercised in our experiment at such a late stage?

However, a word of caution is in order here, especially to novices. The emphasis in psychology on the retrospective evaluation of one's own experiment for design flaws is in many respects an extremely healthy one. However, it can cause problems, especially when your findings are unexpected, and particularly if they contradict established findings/ideas in the area. Under these circumstances many of you lapse into what I call the 'chemistry experiment' mentality. That is, when the results don't come out as predicted, you assume that the experiment hasn't 'worked' and search for where you went 'wrong' – just like we used to when our test-tubes of noxious substances failed to behave as anticipated in chemistry classes (which, as I recall, was most of the time). This is *not* the way to proceed. It may well be that a flaw in your experimental design has produced 'anomolous' results. However, you should not automatically assume that this is the case. As a general rule, *believe* your findings until you discover a feature of your design or procedure that casts doubt upon their validity.

It is not for nothing that this section is called a *Discussion* section, for your task at this stage is to *discuss* the possible explanations of your findings, arriving where possible at a decision as to which of these (for clearly stated reasons) appears to be the most plausible. That is, especially as you become more experienced, you should find yourself elaborating and evaluating a *number* of potential explanations for your findings at this stage, rather than glibly trotting out the one you favour.

For instance, on looking at your experiment you may be struck by an obvious explanation for your findings. Where you have rejected the null hypothesis and the results are in the direction predicted by your experimental hypothesis, then an obvious candidate here is the theory that led you to design and run your experiment in the first place. At other times, it may be the discovery of an obvious confounding variable. Whatever the case, *beware* of this. In psychology experiments there is generally no such thing as *the* explanation. As you should have gathered from our discussion of *statistical inference* (section 10.2) academic psychology is a *probabilistic* enterprise. We can never be absolutely sure that what we believe to be the case is actually the case. So never sound definite where you only really have grounds to be tentative, and always bear in mind that there will probably be alternative explanations for your findings even on those occasions in which the explanation you favour seems so obvious to you as to be undeniably true. Equally, you should also consider the possibility that your DV may still be under the control of your IV even in an experiment which was very badly controlled. (The lack of control makes it difficult for you to establish whether this is the case.)

If your experiment has been reasonably well designed, at the end of this process you should be in a position to say how likely it is that any differences between your conditions were caused by your manipulation of the independent variable, or that the absence of such a difference indicates the lack of a causal relationship between the independent and dependent variables. This is, of course, what the whole enterprise is about. This is why you spend so much time attempting to control for confounding variables – why you employ within subjects variables whenever you can in order to eliminate individual differences, or otherwise attempt to minimize their impact by matching your subjects or, at the very least, by allocating them randomly to conditions. So, if at the end of this phase of your DISCUSSION you are unable to decide about the impact of your independent variable on your dependent variable with *reasonable* confidence there are obviously design lessons to be learnt from your experiment. So learn them! (If at this stage your findings remain equivocal, one question you might think about is whether a *pilot-test* of your experiment would have enabled you to forsee and avoid the problems you encountered, Section 9.10.)

### 5.3 What are the implications of these findings?

In a sense the first two phases of the DISCUSSION are really preliminaries for what is to follow. Having decided what it is we have to explain, and having arrived at our best candidate for the explanation, we can now get to the nitty gritty – assessing the implications of our experiment for the work we outlined in our INTRODUCTION. What, if anything, have we learned about the independent variable from our experiment? Does this advance our ideas in any way, or at least qualify them? To what extent can our findings be reconciled with the theoretical ideas we discussed in the INTRODUCTION? Indeed, do they enable us to decide between any competing theories?

You can see here the close relationship that exists between the DISCUSSION and the INTRODUCTION. Essentially, your task now is to return to the material you addressed in your INTRODUCTION with the benefit of the findings of your study. So, what you are able to say at this crucial stage of your report depends critically on how well you prepared the ground in your INTRODUCTION. A good DISCUSSION, therefore, critically depends upon an adequate INTRODUCTION. Indeed, unless something particularly unforeseeable has occurred, you should find yourself addressing the same themes here as in your INTRODUCTION, albeit with additional knowledge. In general, there should be no need to introduce new evidence from the psychological literature to this section.

Once you have done this you should think about the direction that *future* work might take. This is particularly important when your study has failed to resolve some outstanding problems and issues. At this stage you might suggest problems that need now to be addressed and, if possible, ways in which this might be done.

This is all very well, of course, if your findings have turned out to have been reasonably unequivocal. But what if it has not been possible to say much at all about the relationship between the Independent and Dependent Variables? If this has occurred because of design flaws, then you should go some way towards improving your reputation as a designer of experiments here by indicating ways in which future experiments on the same topic might overcome the difficulties you encountered.

### 5.4 What to do when you've been unable to analyse your data properly

Sometimes, however, these problems will have arisen because you experienced considerable difficulties with your study, difficulties (such as low numbers of subjects) that render your data effectively unanalysable. This, of course, will make writing the DISCUSSION that much more difficult. Whenever possible, try to avoid such circumstances *prior* to running the study. However, such things can happen even when the study has been well thought out in advance. In such instances, when it comes to writing the report, the important thing is to *be seen to have made an effort*.

Do not, therefore, jump at the opportunity (as you see it) of only having to write a brief and dismissive DISCUSSION, but write as thoughtfully as you would have done in the presence of suitably analysed data. Indeed, one of the most effective ways around this problem is not only to examine *carefully* the reasons for the inadequacies in the data (together with the ways in which such occurrences might be avoided in future work), but to actively explore the sorts of implications that your data would have held had the results: (a) turned out as expected and (b) contrary to expectation. At least in doing this you will be able to demonstrate your reasoning skills to your marker – as well as being able to practise them for yourself.

Finally, one of the aspects of the implications of your findings that you should bear in mind concerns their *generalizability*.

## 5.5   The generalizability of findings

All studies have limits on their **generalizability**. That is, on the extent to which we can extrapolate the findings to situations other than those directly assessed in the study itself. In some cases these limitations are severe. In others, they are not. Yet these limitations are often among the first things to be forgotten when studies are discussed in general terms.

Many factors can contribute to the generalizability of a study's findings: the equipment and subjects used, procedure employed, instructions given etc. And one particularly potent source of such limitations can come from the level at which *controlled* values were held constant. For example, if you undertake an experiment in which you control for gender by using only male subjects, then perhaps the data is applicable only to males. Or, if you run an experiment in which you test the effects of alcohol on driving performance using subjects who are only occasional drinkers, then perhaps the findings will not apply to those who drink alcohol more regularly.

*SAQ 24*
For instance, at one Open University Summer School we run an experiment to test whether people can taste the difference between mineral water and tap water. Invariably we find that most people cannot. However, the water is usually kept at room temperature (i.e. the variable *temperature* is *controlled*). Does this mean that we can conclude that people in general cannot taste the difference between mineral water and tap water?

The generalizability of findings is one of the more neglected issues in experimental psychology. It seems likely that the findings of many studies have been *over* generalized. As students, this is one issue that it will be important to think about in *all* aspects of your course, not just your practical work. But in the practical course, spare a thought for this issue when evaluating the studies you include in your

INTRODUCTION and, of course, bear this in mind when assessing your own findings in the DISCUSSION.

*SAQ 25*
What is the purpose of the DISCUSSION?

Finally, here are some tips to help you avoid some common failings in this section:

1. Outline your findings (i.e. the contents of your RESULTS) in the opening paragraph. It is then clear both to yourself and your reader what is to be discussed.
2. Do not repeat material you have covered – or *should* have covered – in the INTRODUCTION. In this section you can assume that your reader has a knowledge of the relevant literature – after all, it was you who gave it to him/her. Where there are gaps in his/her knowledge that make it difficult to conduct your argument, and where these are not the result of unforeseeable (not *unforeseen*) factors influencing your findings, then the gaps are of your own making and reflect omissions from your INTRODUCTION.
3. Include a final paragraph summarizing your main conclusions. But be careful to distinguish between conclusions and mere restatements of findings.
4. Do not confuse *significance* (which refers to the *statistical* nature of the results) with *meaningfulness*: we can often draw meaningful conclusions from non-significant data, and vice versa. Neither confuse significance with *proof*: significant results do not *prove* that the theoretical underpinnings of your study are sound, nor do non-significant results necessarily *disprove* your arguments. Life would be much simpler if they did, but unfortunately this isn't the case; in either instance you will still have to justify your point of view in the DISCUSSION.

*Summary of Sections 5.1–5.5*

1. You should open the DISCUSSION by summarizing the main features of the RESULTS, so that it is clear both to yourself and the reader what it is you feel you have to explain in the DISCUSSION.
2. Once this has been done, you should then search for the best available explanation of the results, examining and assessing the likely candidates in order to arrive at an overall assessment

of what your findings have to tell us about the existence or otherwise of a causal relationship between the IV(s) and the DV(s) in your experiment.

3. These two stages are the necessary preliminaries for the final phase of the DISCUSSION, in which you assess the implications of your findings for the area as outlined in the INTRODUCTION. At the same time you should think about the direction and form that future work might take.

4. Where your findings have been too ambiguous to do this, then you should examine both why this has been the case and ways in which the problems you encountered might be avoided in future work.

5. Finally, you should include a final paragraph summarizing your main conclusions.

Below are two sample Discussions, one for the Cheese and Nightmare experiment, and one for the Mnemonic experiment. These are only suggestions as to how you might go about writing discussions for these sections, and in some respects they provide only *outlines* of what might be argued.

### The Cheese and Nightmare experiment
### Discussion

The results are consistent with the experimental hypothesis: those who consumed cheese three hours before retiring to bed reported a greater number of nightmares than those who did not eat cheese during this time.

Perhaps the most obvious explanation for this finding is the one embodied in folk-wisdom – that eating cheese before going to bed leads to the experience of nightmares. It may be that one or more of the ingredients in cheese affects the human nervous system in a manner that provokes the production of nightmares. However, there are other possible explanations for the above finding that also require consideration.

In the first place, it may well be that it is the *awareness* of being in an experiment concerned with the relationship between cheese and nightmares that is the critical variable here. For, although no subject was actually informed of the precise purpose of the experiment, those in the cheese condition were required to eat a measured quantity of cheese at a specified time and to report subsequently the number of nightmares that they experienced. It is entirely possible that this configuration of tasks enabled them to determine the intent of the experimenter. Consequently, these subjects might have experienced an increase in the incidence of nightmares purely because this was 'suggested' by the structure of the experiment itself. On the other hand, the awareness that they were in an experiment of this nature might simply have led subjects in the experimental condition to *report* a higher incidence of nightmares than they actually experienced.

Unfortunately, it is not possible to assess the extent of 'subject awareness' in this experiment, as the de-briefing sessions failed to explore this question. Future work should therefore check on this possibility and, if possible, less reliance should be placed simply on subjects' verbal *reports* of nightmares. Instead these should be combined with some psychophysiological measurement of, for example, subjects 'rapid eye movements' (REM) sleep.

Another possibility worthy of note concerns whether or not the two groups simply differed in that the cheese condition contained more of those who were likely to experience nightmares anyway. Although some control was made for this possibility by the random allocation of subjects to conditions, it remains possible that the groups did differ in basic proneness to nightmares. One way around this problem might be to employ a within subjects design, comparing subjects' experiences of nightmares on days when they consumed cheese with their experiences on days when they did not. However, such a design might be even more susceptible to the *demand characteristics* (i.e. cues that communicate the experimental hypothesis to the subject) outlined above. A more feasible alternative, therefore, might be simply to assess the *baseline* for each subject by assessing the frequency with which they experience nightmares during a reasonable period *prior* to their participation in the experiment. The impact of cheese upon the incidence of nightmares could then be assessed in relation to this baseline for each subject.

It is not possible, therefore, to unequivocally attribute the increased incidence of nightmares in the cheese condition to the consumption of cheese. However, it remains possible, of course, that it indeed was the cheese that led to the increase in nightmares in the experimental group. If this is shown to be so, further research might then be expended on attempting to establish which of the ingredients of cheese is active in facilitating the production of nightmares. The isolation of such an ingredient might not only help in the reduction of such unpleasant experiences (particularly if it is found to be common to a number of foodstuffs) but may also provide us with further insights into the brain's chemistry.

*The Mnemonic experiment*
### Discussion
Although those in the mnemonic condition recalled more items overall than those in the no-mnemonic group, *both* groups appear to have recalled more items from the easy-to-image list than from the hard-to-image one. Thus, although there is some support here for the experimental hypothesis (in so far as those employing the mnemonic did recall more items than those not employing it, and more items from the easy-to-image list), the absence of a significant interaction between condition and item-type makes unequivocal interpretation of these

69

data difficult. For it appears that there is something about the words in the easy-to-image list that makes them easier to recall regardless of whether someone is employing a mnemonic device.

One possibility that springs to mind is that the two lists simply were not equivalent, even though attempts were made to match the items in both lists for frequency and length. It is not clear, however, in what regards other than imageability the two lists differed.

Moreover, it must be borne in mind that the mnemonic-group did recall more items than the no-mnemonic group. This suggests that at least something about the mnemonic facilitated recall. It may be, for instance, that imageability *per se* enhances item recall, and the provision of a coherent framework in the form of a mnemonic-device that exploits this imageability capitalizes upon this. On the other hand, perhaps it is simply that those using a mnemonic-device are *oriented* towards the imageability of the items and hence attend to the feature that will most facilitate an item's recall. Even so, such arguments would not contradict Korman's (1897) assertion that it was imageability that held the key to the impact of the *method of loci* upon recall.

In this respect, therefore, the results of this experiment appear to be more consistent with those of Korman (1897) and Richards (1984) than with those of Johnson *et al.*, (1985). It seems that the failure of Johnson *et al.*, (1985) to find any effect of the nature of their material upon their subjects' ability to recall lists of words using the *method of loci* stemmed from their failure to allow these subjects to become practised in the use of this technique.

If we accept the central role of imageability here, however, then how do we account for the fact that the recall of the mnemonic-group was superior to that of the no mnemonic-group in hard-to-image items as well as in easy-to-image ones? Why should the mnemonic-group have had their recall of non-imageable items enhanced?

It may be that this is evidence against the proposition that it is imageability that lies at the heart of the facilitation of recall by the *method of loci*. However, it is possible to go some way towards reconciling this apparent anomoly. It may be, for instance, that subjects were able to form images of semantically unrelated, but phonetically similar, words to those in the hard-to-image list (e.g. 'dove' for 'love'), and were therefore able to effectively code these words using the mnemonic device. Unfortunately, subjects weren't questioned about this during the de-briefing session, so it is not possible to take this further here. Future work might bear this possibility in mind.

# 6   Title and Abstract

Although the TITLE and ABSTRACT are the first items to appear in the report (Figure 1.1), we have left coverage of them until the end. This is partly because you need to understand something of the report's structure and purpose before you can begin to appreciate the nature and function of these sections. It is also because they are invariably better left until later in the writing sequence.

In order to understand the reasons for the form that the TITLE and ABSTRACT take, we need to remind ourselves of the function that these sections serve in a *research* report. They are in fact vital to its research function, for they alert potential readers to the existence of an article of interest to them. In fact, these components are generally extracted from the report and published separately in compendiums of abstracts. Thus it is often on the basis of a title and abstract alone that many readers will decide whether to look up an article or simply ignore it. The TITLE and ABSTRACT, therefore, should summarize the study clear, concisely, and (if possible!) attractively.

## 6.1   Title

The title should be as informative as you can make it within the constraints imposed by its length (no longer than one sentence, although you may include colons or semi-colons). It forms, in fact, the first step in the process of searching the literature. It is to a title that would-be readers turn initially in order to discover whether the work might be of interest to them. You should, therefore, provide sufficient information at this stage to enable them to make this initial decision. So, never be vague in the title. Do not title your report 'Memory', for example, or 'An Experimental Investigation of Recall-aids' but something like 'The Effect of the Imageability of the Words to be Recalled on the Effectiveness of the Method of Loci'.

In experimental studies in most instances you should mention both the IV and the DV in the title. Note also that you should begin the first word of the title, together with all subsequent key-words, with a capital letter.

## 6.2   Abstract

The ABSTRACT constitutes the next stage in the process of searching the literature. Having gathered from the title that an article *may* be of interest, would-be readers will generally turn next to the ABSTRACT in order to decide whether to invest time and energy in reading the report itself. So in this section you should provide enough information to enable them to reach this decision. As well as this, however, you should attempt to be as brief as possible. The whole section, then, involves a compromise between these two aims: an abstract should rarely exceed an average paragraph in length.

Indeed, together with the DISCUSSION, the ABSTRACT is one of the most difficult of the sections to write; even quite experienced students (not to mention the odd member of staff, myself included) continue to encounter difficulties with this section. So don't be too dismayed if your initial attempts meet with failure. Where you experience difficulty with this section, thumb through journal articles to see how the Abstracts have been written there. For there's really a 'feel' to a good abstract that is perhaps best absorbed in this way.

The ABSTRACT falls essentially into three parts: a brief account of what you expected, what you found, and what you concluded.

1. Include only the bare essentials of your design, findings and conclusions. Remember that your task is to provide the minimum amount of information necessary for someone to be able to fully comprehend what you did. In general, there is no need to include those procedural details that might be expected to form part of any well-designed experiment, although *unusual* procedural details, or those relevant to the conclusions, should be briefly mentioned.
2. Omit extraneous details: things such as the number of subjects, for example, can be left out, unless you believe them to be critical in some way to the meaning of the experiment.
3. Keep the ABSTRACT as brief as you can within the limits imposed by the need to make it useful and coherent. It should rarely need to be longer than an average paragraph in length. Always look for ways of condensing this section, therefore, while retaining intelligibility and informativeness.
4. Include one or two final sentences at the end of the AB-STRACT outlining your main conclusions. But make sure that you are including those conclusions that you actually arrived at in your DISCUSSION – not ones unrelated to these or 'after-thoughts'.

*SAQ 26*
What functions do the TITLE and ABSTRACT serve in a research report?

*Abstract*

An experiment was conducted to examine whether the usefulness of the *method of loci* mnemonic was influenced by the imageability of the words to be recalled. A group of subjects were given instruction and training in the use of this mnemonic and their recall of items that were easy-to-image and hard-to-image was compared with that of a group of subjects who received no such instruction and training. It was predicted that those using the *method of loci* would recall a greater number of the easy-to-image than the hard-to-image words, and a greater number of the easy-to-image words than those not using this mnemonic. Both predictions were supported by the data, although those not employing the *method of loci* recalled a greater number of the easy-to-image than the hard-to-image words. The possibility that the word lists varied in respects other than imageability was raised, and an attempt made to reconcile these findings with the suggestion that mental imagery is central to the functioning of such mnemonics.

## *Summary of Section 6.1–6.2*

1. In a research report the TITLE and ABSTRACT serve to alert potential readers to an article that might be of interest.
2. They should, therefore, summarize the study clearly, concisely, and attractively.
3. The TITLE should be a sentence in length, the ABSTRACT no longer than an average paragraph.

# 7  *References and Appendices*

## 7.1  *The references section*

This is one of the most neglected sections of the report. Do *not* neglect this section, as it helps to round off the report in style.

In journal articles, this section is an accurate list of all the citations that have been made in the text. In essays and practical reports (*but not final year projects however*) this section is more usually a list of the *sources* you have used in writing the piece (e.g. text-books). In this instance, therefore, a book may appear in your REFERENCES section *even though* you have not cited it in the text (e.g. your course text-book) and vice versa. At this stage it is accepted that you will be dealing mainly with **secondary sources** (i.e. reading other people's accounts of the work of their fellow researchers) and it would be misleading for you to include all the work you cite in the text in your REFERENCES section. So, as a general rule in practical reports, cite only the sources that you yourself *read* when writing the report in your REFERENCES.

### 7.2   General points about references

1. Your references should be in alphabetical order, commencing with the first author's surname and taking each letter in turn.
2. Place *all* single publications by an author *before* his or her *joint* publications (e.g. Reagan, R. would come before Reagan, R. and Gorbachov, M., Reagan, R. and Gorbachov, M., before Reagan, R. and Reagan, N.).
3. With *multiple* publications by the same author(s), place them in *chronological* order (e.g. Healey, D. and Benn, A. (1966) should appear before Healey, D. and Benn, A. (1981)).

### 7.3   Citing books

There is a standard format for referencing different types of publications; that for books is as follows:

Author's surname(s); author's initial(s); date of publication (in brackets); title of book (underlined); place of publication: name of publisher.

> e.g. MITCHELL, N. (1981) *Social Attribution; a primer in obvious psychology* London: Macmillan.

### 7.4   Citing articles in books

Author's surname(s); author's initial(s); date of publication (in brackets); title of article; initial(s) of editor(s); surname(s) of editor(s); date of publication of book (if different); title of book (underlined); place of publication: name of publisher.

e.g. Botham, I. T. and Argyle, M. (1972) 'Staring you in the face' in M. Thatcher (ed) (1980) *If it had teeth: 15 years of research into non-verbal communication* New York: Academic Press.

## 7.5 Citing journal articles

Author's surname(s); author's initial(s); date of publication (in brackets); title of article; journal title (underlined); journal volume number (underlined); inclusive page numbers.

e.g. Brown, A. and Green, A. (1974) 'The effects of locus of control on attributions for performance outcomes among junior high school pupils' *The Journal of Tedious Research, 52,* pp 317–324.

## 7.6 Appendices

Many students' reports seem to have had almost as much effort expended on the **appendices** as on the rest of the report. This is invariably a waste of effort as appendices are rarely examined in any detail by your tutors – and when they are this is usually because you have included in this section something that should have appeared in the body of the report. The purpose of appendices is essentially to enable you to expand on information that you have been able to include only in abbreviated form in the body of the report itself. *But all vital information should appear in the report, not here!* So, include in this section things like the verbatim instructions (when these are too long to include the full text in the PROCEDURE); a copy of the questionnaire you used in your study; examples of the stimulus cards or lists of words you used etc. But make sure that vital information is not mentioned here for the first time!

## Check list for report writing

1. Avoid mentioning things 'in passing' – if they are worth mentioning at all, then give them the amount of space they deserve.
2. Make your points *explicitly*; do not leave it to your reader to work out what you mean. Be precise *at all times*. Never assume that the reader knows something, or expect the reader to work something important out for his or her self.

3. Do not use note-form at *any* stage of the report: *prose* is always required.
4. Use the same tense and case throughout – preferably the third person, past impersonal; e.g. 'It was found that . . .', 'The sheets were administered . . .', etc. (But see section 1.3.)
5. Omit extraneous details: always look for ways of condensing the information that you give, within the limits imposed by comprehension.
6. *Do not waffle* – unnecessary repetition is both tedious and obvious and is unlikely to impress the person marking your report (quite the opposite).
7. Tell the truth!

### What the marker's looking for

One of the most daunting things about report and essay writing is the fact that you're often not at all clear exactly what the marker is expecting of you. In a sense, of course, the whole of this book is an attempt to help you with this problem. But, in addition, below is a summary of *some* of the questions with which the marker might address your report. Note, however, that some of these requirements are rather more important than others.

### Title

Does this convey a clear and accurate idea of what the study was about?
Does it mention the major variables investigated?

### Abstract

Does this convey a clear and accurate idea of what the study was about?
Is it clear what the findings were?
Is intelligible reference made to the contents of the DISCUSSION?
Is a conclusion mentioned, and is this the one actually arrived at?
Can you understand the ABSTRACT without referring to the report itself?
Is it concise enough, or does it include unnecessary detail?

## Introduction

### Part 1

Is the study introduced adequately, given the student's background? In particular, is there an adequate review of the relevant background literature?
Is there a logical progression to the Introduction? Does it *build up* to an account of the study undertaken?
Does the study have sufficient research justification? (Where applicable)

### Part 2

Is the study described adequately and accurately? In particular, is there a clear statement of the predictions, and are these justified?

## Method

### Design

Is the design described thoroughly and accurately?
Are the IVs described thoroughly and accurately, including a clear description of the levels?
Are the DVs described thoroughly and accurately, including a clear account of the units of measurement?
Has the design been labelled correctly?
Is the correct terminology used?

### Subjects

Are the subjects described adequately?
Are there sufficient?
Are they appropriate for this type of study?
Have they been allocated to groups properly?
Were they selected reasonably?

### Apparatus and/or Materials

Is this section properly labelled?
Is the equipment used described in the kind of detail that would enable an *exact* replication to be undertaken?

*Procedure*

Is this described in enough detail to allow for an exact replication?
Is it clear how the procedure differed for the different conditions?
Are the instructions reported adequately?
Were they suitable?
Was sufficient attempt made to ensure that the subjects understood the instructions?
Were the subjects treated reasonably?
Were they de-briefed?
Was deception used and, if so, was this justifiable and well handled?
Does the procedure have flaws that render interpretation of the data difficult?

*Results*

Is it clear what data was analysed and how the numbers presented in the tables of data were arrived at?
Are the data adequately described and clearly presented?
Are tables labelled appropriately and readily intelligible?
Is it clear what statistics were used in any given instance?
Is it clear what was found?
Is the necessary information provided with each test?
Has the statistical criterion been adhered to?
Has the data been used to good effect?
Has the data been presented intelligently and well? In particular, were the results presented in a logical order?
Has the student resisted the temptation to *interpret* the findings at this stage?

*Discussion*

Are the findings summarized intelligently and accurately?
Have they been interpreted sensibly?
Are the obvious interpretations of these findings discussed?
Are any other interpretations discussed?
Is the discussion sensible and balanced?
Have any inconsistencies or contradictions in the findings been addressed?
Has enough attempt been made to assess the implications of the findings for the material reviewed in the INTRODUCTION?

Does the DISCUSSION include an account of any flaws in the design that might have affected the data?
Have the broader implications of the findings been mentioned, and are these sensible?
Is there any discussion of the implications for future research?
Are any conclusions drawn? Are these sensible?

## References

Is this section properly laid out, and does it contain the appropriate references?

## Miscellaneous

Have the conventions of report writing been properly observed'?
Docs the material appear in the proper sections?
Are references made for factual assertions, and is this properly done?
Are any tables, figures, quotations etc., properly constructed and referenced?
Would the report be comprehensible to someone who had no knowledge of the study, or the area of psychology in which it took place?

# Part 2
# Principles of Experimental Design

# 8   *Experimenting in Psychology*

The report as described in Part 1 is primarily designed for the reporting of *experiments*. This method of collecting data is the one most widely employed by psychologists. However, there are other techniques available, such as the *correlation*, or even simple *description*. It is now time to consider these techniques in some detail.

The first term you must learn here is the term **variable**. In the language of design we tend to use this as a noun – that is we talk of 'a variable' or 'the variable'. To us, a variable is quite simply something – anything – that *varies*. All around us there are variables: people come in *different* shapes and sizes, belong to *different* groups and classes, have *different* abilities and tastes. As researchers we can ask the subjects in our experiments to do *different* things – to learn different lists of words for a memory test, to do boring or interesting tasks, to do press-ups for three minutes or spend the same amount of time relaxing. All of these things – from social class through to whether our subjects did press-ups or relaxed – are *variables*. For a variable is quite simply something that isn't always the same, that can come in different forms. So, in the above example social class is a variable because there are *different* social classes; doing different tasks is also a variable because the task varies – it can be *either* interesting *or* boring. As our world is full of changing events, therefore, it is no surprise to find that almost anything in it is – or can be – a variable.

A variable, then, is something that can come in different forms or, as we say in design terms, that can take different *values*. In practice it can be anything from the number of white blood cells in a cubic centimetre of blood to whether or not someone voted Conservative at the last General Election. In our scientific hats we are extremely interested in variables, especially in finding out something about relationships *between* them.

Our ultimate aim is to find out which variables are responsible for *causing* the events that take place around us. We see a world full of variables and we want to know what factors are responsible for producing or *causing* them. Why is it that some people react with depression to events that others take in their stride? Why is it that some public speakers are more persuasive than others? What makes one list of words easier to recall than another? We believe that we live in a universe of causes and effects and our adopted task is to try to determine, as far as is possible, which are the causes and what are the effects they produce. That is, ideally we want to be able to infer cause and effect relationships, to make what are known as **causal infer-**

**ences**. Our principal weapon in this battle is the psychological *experiment*.

## 8.1  The experiment

In an **experiment** what we do – quite simply – is play around with one variable (the one we suspect to be the **causal variable**), and see what happens to another variable (the one that is the **effect variable**). That is, as experimenters we deliberately alter the **values** or **levels** of the causal variable – or, as we say in experimental design parlance, we **manipulate this variable** – and look to see if this produces corresponding changes in the other – the effect – variable. If it does, and we cannot see any other variable in the situation that may have produced this effect, we assume that the variable we have manipulated has indeed produced the change we observed. That is, we infer a cause–effect relationship between the two variables (i.e. make a *causal inference*). This is the logic of experimental design.

For instance, if we suspected that eating foods which contained particular additives was responsible for causing certain types of depression, we would *vary* the intake of these additives among our subjects and see whether this produced any corresponding changes in the incidence of depression. That is, we would *manipulate* the variable food additives and *measure* the variable depression. Similarly, if we wanted to find out whether physical exercise affected mental alertness, we would *manipulate* the variable physical exercise and *measure* the variable mental alertness. In the above examples, food additives and physical exercise are the variables we suspect to be *causal*; depression and mental alertness the variables we think they influence.

However, because they are both variables, and yet play quite distinct roles in an experiment, we give these critical variables different names. The one we play around with – the variable we manipulate – we call the **Independent Variable** (IV). The independent variable, therefore, is the variable that we suspect is the *causal* variable. The variable we look at to see if there are any changes produced by our manipulation of the causal variable – that is, the variable we *measure* – we call the **Dependent Variable** (DV). The dependent variable, therefore, is the variable that shows us whether there is any effect of changing the values of the independent variable. If there is such an effect, then the values the dependent variable takes will *depend* on the values that we, as experimenters, set *independently* on our independent variable.

It is important that you get this straight. These terms are critical and you will need to apply them properly in your report. So read back through the last paragraph carefully, and then answer the following questions.

*SAQ 27*
In an experiment:
(a) What is the name of the variable we *manipulate*?
(b) What is the name of the variable we *measure*?
For each of the following experiments, write down what the *independent variable* is and what the *dependent variable* is:

a. An experimenter is interested in the effect of word frequency upon the time taken to decide whether a stimulus is a *word* or a *non-word* (a meaningless combination of vowels and consonants). S/he exposes the same set of subjects to three sets of words which vary in their frequency (High, Medium, and Low) and measures the time it takes them to decide whether they have seen a word or a non-word in milliseconds.

b. A researcher is interested in the effect of the sex hormone oestrogen on the feeding behaviour of female rats. S/he injects one group with a suitable concentration of oestrogen and another group with an equivalent volume of saline solution. After three days s/he measures the changes that have taken place in their body weights in grammes.

c. A social psychologist is interested in the role that anxiety plays in persuasion. S/he develops three separate public information programmes on dental care. These programmes vary in the extent to which they arouse anxiety in their viewers: one provokes a comparatively high level of anxiety, another a moderate degree of anxiety, and the third comparatively little anxiety. S/he exposes three separate groups of subjects to these programmes and then assesses how many of those in each of the three groups subsequently take up the opportunity to make a dental appointment.

d. An experimenter is interested in the effects of television violence upon the level of aggression it induces in its viewers. S/he exposes three separate groups of subjects to three different kinds of television programme: one in which the violence is 'realistic' (i.e. the blows cause obvious damage to the recipients), one in which the violence is 'unrealistic' (i.e. the blows do not appear to damage the recipient, or hinder his ability to continue fighting), and one in which no violence is portrayed. The subjects are subsequently allowed to administer electric shocks to their own victims during the course of a simulated teaching exercise (although, unbeknown to them, no actual shocks are delivered). The experimenter measures the mean level of shock (in volts) administered by those in each of the three groups.

e. An occupational psychologist wishes to examine the impact of working with others on the productivity of a group of factory workers. S/he measures the number of packets of breakfast cereal this group pack into boxes in a 20 minute period when: a. working alone, b. working with one other worker, c. working with two others, d. working with four others, and e. working with eight others.

As experimenters we only control the values of the *independent variable*; we have no control over the precise values taken by the *dependent variable*. You will obtain these latter values from your *subjects*; things like reaction times (in milliseconds), number of errors made, personality scale scores (e.g. scores for Extraversion on the Eysenck Personality Inventory), blood glucose level (e.g. in milligrams per 100 millilitres) etc. And note that you must *always* mention the units in which your dependent variable was measured.

## Summary of Section 8.1

1. A variable is anything that can come in different forms. In experiments variables are manipulated in order to see what effects this has on other variables, in other words which variables *cause* changes in other variables.
2. The variable we *manipulate* in an experiment is known as the *Independent Variable* (IV).
3. The variable we *measure* in an experiment to see if our IV manipulation has caused any changes is known as the *Dependent Variable* (DV).

## 8.2 Experimental and control conditions

When we *manipulate* an independent variable, therefore, what we do is alter the *values* or *levels* it takes. We then look to see if altering these levels produces any corresponding changes in the subjects' scores – the *dependent variable*. The different values or levels of the independent variable we call the *conditions* of our experiment. What we are interested in doing is *comparing* these conditions to see if there are any differences between them in the subjects' scores. This, in a nutshell, is the logic of experimental design. Now let's see how it all looks in a real experiment.

Suppose I am interested in 'folk wisdom' – and, in particular, in the old adage that eating cheese shortly before going to bed gives you nightmares. One basic way we might test this proposition experimentally would be to take two groups of people, give one group a measured quantity of cheese (say in proportion to their body weight) a standard time before going to bed (say 3 hours) and ensure that those in the other group consumed no cheese during the same period. We could then count the number of nightmares reported by the two groups.

*SAQ 28*
What are the independent and dependent variables in this experiment?

In this case we have manipulated our independent variable (cheese consumption) by forming two *conditions*: one in which the subjects eat cheese (condition 1), and one in which they do not eat cheese (condition 2). We are interested in the consequences of this – in the effect that this will have on the number of nightmares the subjects in the two conditions experience.

This is a very basic experimental design. Our manipulation of the independent variable in this case involves comparing what happens when the suspected causal variable (cheese) is *present* (condition 1) with what happens when it is *absent* (condition 2). If cheese *does* cause nightmares, then we would expect those in condition 1 to experience more nightmares than those in condition 2. If cheese does *not* cause nightmares, then we should expect no such difference.

There are particular names for the conditions in an experiment where the independent variable is manipulated by comparing its *presence* with its *absence*. The condition in which the suspected causal variable is *present* is called the **experimental condition**. The condition in which the suspected causal variable is *absent* is called the **control condition**.

*SAQ 29*
Which is the *control* condition in the above experiment?

Experiments in which we simply compare an *experimental* with a *control* condition can be simple and effective ways of finding things out in psychology. But such a design does not exhaust the possibilities. We may, for instance, be more interested in comparing the effects of two different *levels* of the independent variable, than in comparing its presence with its absence. For instance, we might be interested in finding out whether different *types* of cheese produce different numbers of nightmares. We might therefore wish to compare a group of subjects who ate Cheddar cheese with a group that ate Caerphilly cheese. In such an experiment, cheese would be present in *both conditions*. We would have therefore an experiment with two *experimental* conditions, rather than a *control* and *experimental* condition.

Such a design is perfectly acceptable in psychology. In fact, we don't even need to restrict ourselves to comparing only *two* experimental conditions – we can compare three or even more in one experiment. And one of these can be a *control* condition if we wish – that is, a condition in which the suspected causal variable is absent. So, for instance, we might expand our cheese and nightmare experiment to one in which we had a group of subjects who ate Cheddar cheese, a group who ate Caerphilly cheese, a group who ate Red

Leicester, a group who ate Cheshire, and a group who ate no cheese at all.

*SAQ 30*
How many conditions are there *overall* in this version of the cheese experiment? How many of these are *experimental* conditions?

*SAQ 31*
Go back through the experiments described in SAQ 27, and state how many conditions each IV has. Do any of these have a *control* condition? If so, which ones?


## 8.3    Control: holding extraneous variables constant

What we do in an experiment, therefore, is manipulate the variable we suspect to be causal – what we have learned to call the independent variable (IV) – and examine what impact this manipulation has upon the effect variable – what we have learned to call the dependent variable (DV). If we subsequently find that there are indeed changes in the dependent variable this strengthens our suspicion that there is a causal link between them.

However, in order to make this *causal inference* we have to ensure that the independent variable really is the only thing that we are changing in the experiment. Thus, in our cheese and nightmare experiment, for example, we don't want more people who are suffering life crises, or taking sleeping-pills, or who are otherwise prone to experiencing nightmares, to end up in the one condition rather than the other. If they did, we would no longer be sure that any differences we observed in our dependent variable (incidence of nightmares) would be due to our manipulation of the cheese variable, or to these other subject-based variables. For, if our groups of subjects indeed varied in their intake of sleeping-pills it might be that this variable (sleeping-pill consumption) is responsible for any differences between the groups in the extent to which they experience nightmares, rather than our independent variable (cheese consumption).

A variable that changes along with our independent variable is always an alternative possible cause of any differences we observe in our dependent variable. It represents a rival explanation for these effects, and is consequently an unwelcome intruder. We must, therefore, attempt to eliminate such **extraneous variables** (extraneous = not belonging to the matter in hand). And we do this by **controlling** for them.

The commonest way of controlling is to hold the other candidates for the causal variable *constant* throughout our experiment, whilst varying the IV alone. Thus, in our cheese and nightmare experiment we would attempt to ensure that the only difference between our groups of subjects was whether or not they ate cheese before going to bed. Consequently, we would do our best to make sure that the groups really did not differ in their sleeping-pill consumption, or life crises – or any other variable that might make them prone to experiencing nightmares.

Uncontrolled variables that change along with our independent variable are known in the trade as **confounding variables** (to confound = to confuse), for they confound the effects of our independent variable. You will find that much of the time you spend on the design of your experiments will actually involve recognizing and controlling for possible confounding variables. For confounding variables prevent us from unequivocally attributing the changes we find in the DV to our manipulation of the IV. This is because they provide possible alternative explanations, e.g. that any differences in the occurrence of nightmares are caused by sleeping-pills, rather than by cheese consumption.

*Summary of Sections 8.2–8.3*

1. An experiment has many *extraneous* variables. In order to design an effective experiment, therefore, we have to isolate the variables we are interested in by holding extraneous variables constant. This is known as *controlling* these other variables.
2. Extraneous variables that we fail to control for are *confounding variables*.
3. An effective experiment does not have confounding variables.

### 8.4 Experimental and null hypotheses

In an experiment, then, we *manipulate* an independent variable by altering the *values* it takes, and simultaneously we *control* other candidates for the causal variable by holding them *constant* across the conditions. We then look to see if the changes we make to the independent variable result in changes to the dependent variable – that is, whether there are *differences* in the dependent variable between our *conditions*. Therefore, we are critically interested in the *outcome* of our experiment – in the effect that our manipulation of the independent variable will have on the dependent variable. In particular, if our independent variable really is the causal variable, then we can anticipate, or *hypothesize*, what the actual outcome will be. This is a fundamental feature of experimenting. It is now time to consider it in some detail.

Think back to the cheese experiment. If folk wisdom is correct, then what would we expect to happen in this experiment? Wisdom has it that eating cheese shortly before going to sleep will result in nightmares. Therefore, we should expect those in the cheese condition to experience more nightmares than those in the control condition. That is, if cheese really does cause nightmares then we would expect more of those who eat cheese before going to bed to experience nightmares than those who do not eat cheese before going to bed.

*SAQ 32*
But is this the only possible outcome? What else might happen? Put the book down for a while and think about this clearly.

In fact our experiment can have one of *three* possible outcomes. We might find that *more* nightmares are experienced by those in the experimental than in the control condition. On the other hand, we might find that *fewer* nightmares are experienced by those in the experimental than in the control condition. Finally, we might find that there is essentially *no difference* between the conditions in the number of nightmares the subjects experience. This will be true of *all* experiments in which we test for differences between two conditions; between them, these three options exhaust the possibilities. So – and this is important – we can specify *in advance* what the outcome of our experiment might be.

However, there is an important distinction to be made between these three potential outcomes. Two of them predict that there will be a *difference* between our conditions in the incidence of nightmares. These happen to be the outcomes that we would anticipate *if* cheese affects nightmares in some way (either by stimulating or suppressing them). The third outcome, however, is that there will be no noteworthy difference between them. This is what we would expect if cheese had no influence upon nightmares.

Thus, if we assume that cheese *does* affect the occurrence of nightmares in some way, we would predict – or *hypothesize* – a different outcome to our experiment than if we assumed that cheese had no effect upon the incidence of nightmares. That is, if we assume that cheese in some way changes the likelihood of experiencing nightmares, we would hypothesize that there will be a difference of some sort between our groups in the frequency with which they report nightmares. And the assumption that cheese influences the occurrence of nightmares is, of course, the very assumption that led us to design our experiment in the first place. So, under the assumption that led to the experiment, we would predict a difference of some sort between our two groups. For this reason we call this expectation our **experimental hypothesis**. In fact:

1. *All* experiments have experimental hypotheses.
2. These hypotheses *always* predict a difference between conditions i.e. they predict a difference as a result of manipulating the levels of the independent variable.

*SAQ 33*
Go back to SAQ 27 and work through the examples there, stating what you think the experimental hypotheses might be.

Now, experimental hypotheses come in one of two forms. There is the **bi-directional experimental hypothesis**, which states that there will be a difference somewhere between the conditions in your experiment, but says nothing about the *direction* of this difference (i.e. does not state which condition will exceed the other on the DV). And there is the **uni-directional experimental hypothesis**, which not only predicts the occurrence of such a difference, but also says something about the direction that difference will take.

Thus, in our cheese and nightmare experiment, the bi-directional experimental hypothesis simply states that the experimental and control group will experience *different* numbers of nightmares. A uni-directional experimental hypothesis, on the other hand, would state for example that our cheese group will experience *more* nightmares than our no-cheese group. If we adopt a uni-directional experimental hypothesis, however, we cannot have it both ways. For instance, if we choose to predict that our cheese group will have a higher incidence of nightmares than our no-cheese group, we are *automatically* precluding the possibility that our cheese group will have a lower incidence of nightmares than our no-cheese group. If we don't wish to do this, then we must adopt a bi-directional experimental hypothesis.

*SAQ 34*
These hypotheses are sometimes also referred to as **directional** and **non-directional experimental hypotheses**. Can you think which one is also known as a *directional* experimental hypothesis?

But what of the third possible outcome – the prediction that there will be *no difference* between the two conditions? This is a very important prediction and takes a name of its own. It is called the **null hypothesis** (null = amounting to nothing) and it plays a crucial role in the process by which you come to analyse your data (the 'null' refers to the difference, not the hypothesis!). In fact:

1. *All* experiments have a null hypothesis.
2. This null hypothesis is *always* the same. It is the prediction that there will be *no-difference* on your dependent variable between the conditions in your experiment.

It is, in fact, the prediction based on the assumption that your independent variable does *not* affect your dependent variable. It is a critical hypothesis for, at the end of your experiment, following the analysis of your data, you will be obliged to make a decision. This decision will concern the actual outcome of your experiment. And it will take the form of the decision whether to *accept* the null hypothesis or to *reject* it.

Now it is very important that you do not confuse these two hypotheses. An experimental hypothesis *always* predicts some form of difference. Similarly, the null hypothesis is *always* a prediction of no difference. You can never design an experiment in which your *experimental* hypothesis predicts that there will be no difference between your conditions. To do so is actually to fail to test your theoretical ideas (See Appendix 1).

This is why it is important not to think of your experimental hypothesis as the *experimenter's personal* hypothesis. It is perfectly conceivable that you might design and run an experiment in which you don't really expect there to be a difference between your conditions (e.g. if you're testing a theory that you don't agree with). But the experimental hypothesis would still predict a difference, even if this wasn't the hypothesis you favoured or expected. For instance, I might be sceptical about the validity of folk wisdom and thus expect (privately) that I will find no difference in the incidence of nightmares in my two conditions of eating or not eating cheese. Nevertheless, my *experimental* hypothesis will be the prediction of such a difference. For this is the proposition under test in the experiment.

*Summary of Section 8.4*

1. All experiments have at least one experimental hypothesis and one null hypothesis.
2. The experimental hypothesis is based on the assumption that the independent variable affects the dependent variable. It is

*always* the prediction that there will be a *difference* on the dependent variable somewhere among the conditions in the experiment.

3. The experimental hypothesis can either predict a difference between conditions in one direction (uni-directional) or in either direction (bi-directional).

5. The null hypothesis is based on the assumption that the independent variable does *not* affect the dependent variable. It is the same in all experiments. It predicts the *absence* of a difference among the conditions in the experiment.

## 8.5 Correlations

Most of your practical work in psychology will probably involve experimenting. Consequently, most of this guide is concerned with designing and reporting experiments. But there are other types of study that you might undertake and have to report. For it is not always possible to conduct experiments. There may, for instance, be practical or ethical factors that prevent us from actually *manipulating* variables in the way we need for our studies to qualify as experiments. Under such circumstances we can turn to a rather less powerful, but still informative, technique – the **correlation**.

The critical difference between the experiment and the correlation is that with a correlation we are unable to distinguish between *independent* and *dependent* variables. This is because we do not *manipulate* variables when we undertake a correlation. Instead we rely on *natural* changes to tell us something about which variables are related in some way to each other.

For instance, suppose that we were interested in whether the consumption of saturated fats was a principal cause of heart disease. There would be profound ethical objections to the obvious experiment here: to allocate individuals from birth to diets that were either high or low in their saturated fat content, and then to compare the numbers in each group that eventually contracted heart disease. Under these circumstances, if we wish to gather data on humans, then we are restricted to *correlational* data. In this instance we rely on differences that exist already in the population. That is, we would look to see if there were any correspondence between the amount of saturated fat people ate and the incidence of heart disease. However, this has profound implications for our ability to say anything about the *nature* of the relationship between the variables saturated fat consumption and heart disease.

For instance, suppose that we did indeed find that there was a relationship between them – that, as the consumption of saturated fat increased, so did the incidence of heart disease. This we would call a **positive correlation** (positive because *increases* in the consumption of saturated fat are accompanied by *increases* in the incidence of heart disease.) Such a relationship is depicted graphically in Figure 8.1.

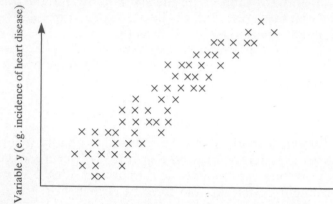

Variable x (e.g. Consumption of saturated fat)

**Figure 8.1** A positive correlation

Now, at first glance it seems obvious to conclude that it is the saturated fat that is *causing* the heart disease. However we actually have no grounds for drawing this conclusion. For, with correlational data all we know is that there is an *association* between these variables. It could be that saturated fats *cause* heart disease. But it could also be that something else is responsible for the relationship. For example, perhaps a diet high in saturated fats is also high in salt, and perhaps it is the salt that is responsible for the heart disease. Or perhaps there is something about people who are prone to experiencing heart disease that also makes them like eating diets high in saturated fat. With correlational data we simply cannot tell.

An illustration might reveal this more clearly. There is, in fact, a positive correlation between the consumption of ice-cream and the incidence of deaths by drowning. That is, as people tend to eat more ice-cream, so more people tend to die in drowning accidents.

*SAQ 35*
Does this mean that there must be some kind of causal relationship between them (even if we can't say which way it goes)?

Now this relationship is sufficiently bizarre for us to suspect that something strange is going on. But *even where the direction of causality seems obvious* it is still not permissible to assume that one of the two variables is responsible for causing the changes we observe. For, in relying upon natural changes, rather than manipulating variables, we are unable to control variables that *co-vary* (i.e. vary along) with the ones that we are interested in. That is, we are unable to control for *confounding* variables. So, be aware of this problem – it applies to many issues, even those – such as smoking and lung-cancer, or the consumption of saturated fats and heart disease – in which the direction of causality seems 'obvious'.

As you can see, it's no surprise that the biggest debates in our scientific and public lives often centre around issues for which the data, concerning humans at least, is *correlational*.

## 8.6  *Description*

Finally, rather than concerning ourselves with relationships *between* variables, we may be content simply to *describe* particular variables. For instance, we might wish to examine the nature of people's attitudes towards nuclear warfare, or to find out what they can tell us about some aspect of their social behaviour. Such studies are neither experimental nor correlational. They are *descriptive*.

A classic example of such an approach is the public opinion poll. Opinion polls tell us things like the percentage of the sample questioned who stated that they would be prepared to vote for particular parties if an election were held immediately, or who they thought would make the best Prime Minister or President. This is **description**. It is simply an attempt to make a statement about the characteristics of the variable 'The Voting Public'. But there is no attempt to *explain* these findings. That is, the data themselves are not used to explain *why* the individuals sampled intend to vote the way they do. Data of this nature is usually generated by *questionnaire* or *interview*, take the form of what is called a *survey*, and are described in terms of *descriptive statistics* (things like percentages, means, etc.).

Now there's no need to worry about telling these techniques apart at this stage. The important thing is to bear in mind that the report as illustrated in Figure 1.1 is designed principally for the reporting of *experiments*. The format illustrated there may well require some degree of modification for the reporting of other types of study, particularly *surveys*.

*Summary of Sections 8.5–8.6*

1. The critical difference between the correlation and the experiment is that in the correlation we are unable to distinguish between *independent* and *dependent* variables. This is because we do not *manipulate* any variables in a correlation. Instead, we rely upon differences that already exist to discover which variables are related to each other.
2. The consequence of this is that we are unable to draw *causal inferences* from correlational data. That is, correlations reveal *associations* between variables, rather than causes and effects.
3. The structured sequence of the report's sections shown in Figures 1.1 to 1.4 is designed primarily for writing up reports of *experiments*.

# 9   Experimental Design

Although experiments have a universal *basic* structure, they vary in design and complexity. For instance, they may have one or more than one independent variable, any or all of which may be *between* or *within* subjects variables. It is time to find out what this means.

## 9.1   Experimental designs with one independent variable

Suppose we have been approached by the Ministry of Transport to undertake some research into the effect of listening to car radios and cassettes upon driving performance. There are lots of ways we could go about doing this. For instance, we might examine actual driving performance on the road, or on a test track, or perhaps we could gain access to a driving simulator and test people's performance on that. Similarly, we might examine only certain aspects of driving performance: for example manual control (things like gear changing, driving in the right lane etc.), or average speed. Or we could assess the number of mistakes made over a standard course, or monitor the subjects' eye-movements as they drove to discover whether there were any differences in the way they monitored the situation unfolding outside as a function of having the radio on or off.

On the other hand we might wish to refine the question we explored – examine whether different materials (e.g. different types of music, or different types of radio programme) affected performance in different ways or to a different extent. Similarly, we might examine whether the volume at which we listened was important – and whether this differed with the material being listened to. Or we might be concerned with whether inexperienced drivers were affected more than experienced ones, or men more than women.

All of these possibilities hold different implications for the experiment we would eventually design and the conclusions we would ultimately draw. Essentially, we have here a whole series of decisions we have to make about the *independent variable* (IV or IVs) in our experiment, and the *dependent variable* (DV or DVs). But there's one fundamental feature of our design that – even after we have decided on the precise question we wish to examine, chosen our IV and DV, and set the levels on the IV – we would still have to decide upon. And this is how we will *distribute* the subjects in our experiment.

For instance, suppose we decided to run the above experiment on a driving simulator, using a computer to display a standard set of hazards and problems in a random sequence. We could then measure driving performance on a range of *relevant* measures from average speed through manual control to number of (pretend!) pedestrians knocked over. The subject could be free to choose his/her own listening material and to set the volume and adjust it whenever s/he desired.

So far, so good. But we have yet to decide how we are going to distribute our *subjects* across the different conditions (radio on versus radio off). We could, for example, have one group of subjects performing in the radio-on condition and another (different) group in the radio-off condition. Such a design – one in which we have *different* subjects in each of our experimental conditions – is known in the trade as a **between subjects design**. It is called a *between* subjects design because, when we compare the data from our conditions, we are actually comparing the data from different subjects. Hence, our statistical comparisons are made *between* subjects.

However, instead of assessing the driving performance of different subjects, we could compare the driving performance of the *same* subjects. That is, we could measure each subject's performance when driving with the radio off and his/her performance when driving with the radio on. This latter design – in which we have the same subjects performing in each of our conditions – is known as a **within subjects**

**design**. It is called a within subjects design because now when we compare the data from our different conditions we are actually comparing data from the same subjects. Hence our statistical comparisons are made *within* subjects.

*SAQ 36*
What type of design did we have in our original, two condition cheese experiment? How else could we have run this experiment, and what would this design have been called?

These then are two basic designs used by psychologists: the *between* subjects design, in which we take a different batch of subjects for each of the conditions in our experiment; and the *within* subjects design, in which we use the same batch of subjects throughout. Other names for the *between* subjects design are **unrelated** and **independent**. Other names for the *within* subjects design are **related** and (under certain circumstances) **matched** (see section 10.3). These designs are illustrated in Tables 9.1 and 9.2. You can see that for our between subjects experiment we need 16 subjects to obtain 8 subjects per condition. For our within subjects version, however, we only need 8 subjects to do this.

**Table 9.1**   A between subjects design with two conditions. Subjects have been allocated to conditions randomly.

| Condition 1 | Condition 2 |
| --- | --- |
| s3 | s12 |
| s10 | s9 |
| s5 | s11 |
| s4 | s7 |
| s8 | s13 |
| s16 | s6 |
| s1 | s15 |
| s14 | s2 |

NOTE:
s = subject

Those of you who weren't expected to contribute to the design of your experiment will still need to be able to state what type of design you employed. So you must learn to make the above distinction. But those of you who are expected to contribute at the design stage will also need to be able to decide which design to employ. So now we'll

**Table 9.2**  A within subjects design with two conditions. Orders have been counterbalanced and allocated randomly.

| Subject Number | Condition 1 | Condition 2 |
|:---:|:---:|:---:|
| s1 | 2nd | 1st |
| s2 | 1st | 2nd |
| s3 | 1st | 2nd |
| s4 | 2nd | 1st |
| s5 | 2nd | 1st |
| s6 | 1st | 2nd |
| s7 | 2nd | 1st |
| s8 | 1st | 2nd |

NOTE:
s = subject

*SAQ 37*
Now go back through the experiments outlined in SAQ 27 and state what type of design the experimenters employed in each.


turn to a consideration of the factors to bear in mind when deciding which design to use in your experiment.


*Summary of Section 9.1*

1.  Two basic experimental designs employed in psychology are the *between* (*independent* or *unrelated*) subjects design and the *within* (*matched* or *related*) subjects design.
2.  In the between subjects design, a *different* set of subjects are allocated to each experimental condition.
3.  In the within subjects design, the *same* set of subjects appear in every condition.


### 9.2   *Deciding between within and between subjects designs*

In order to consider how you might choose between these designs, we must think back to the logic of experimental design discussed earlier. The aim is to manipulate the variable we suspect to be causal – what we have learned to call the Independent Variable (IV) – and examine what impact this manipulation has upon the effect variable – what we have learned to call the Dependent Variable (DV). If we find that there are indeed changes in the DV this strengthens our suspicion that there is a causal link between them.

However, as we pointed out earlier, in order to make this causal inference we have to ensure that the IV really is the only thing that we are changing in the situation; i.e. we do not want any *confounding* variables arising from our particular sample of subjects. Thus, in our driving and stereo experiment, for example, we don't want too many more of the better drivers to end up in the one condition rather than the other. For, if they did, we would no longer be sure that any differences we observed in our DV (e.g. number of errors made over a standard course) would be due to our manipulation of the radio variable, or to basic differences in driving ability. Confounding variables, remember, prevent us from unequivocally attributing the changes we find in the DV to our manipulation of the IV, because they provide possible alternative explanations, e.g. that any differences in driving performance in the two conditions is due to basic differences in ability to drive rather than to the effect of having the radio on or off.

Essentially, you will find that the two types of design differ in the nature and extent of their potentially confounding variables.

Let's illustrate this with an example. Suppose we ran our driving and stereo experiment with a *between subjects* design, and found that those who drove with the radio *off* performed better than those who drove with the radio *on*. This could of course be because having the radio on affects concentration and impairs ability to drive. But, as we pointed out earlier, it could also be simply because more of the better drivers were put into the radio off condition. For there are pronounced **individual differences** in driving ability. Any differences in driving performance between groups of *different* people therefore, might well stem from this basic fact of life, rather than from any manipulation of our independent variable. And, in a between subjects design, of course, we are comparing the performances of different people.

Now there are ways in which we can attempt to *minimize* the impact of individual differences upon our experiment. But there is only one way in which we can actually *eliminate* this source of *extraneous* variation. This is by employing a *within subjects* design.

In a within subjects design we do not compare the performances of *different* people. Instead, we compare the performances of the *same* people on different occasions. So, in the case of our stereo experiment we would assess the driving performance of any given individual when driving with the radio on with his/her performances when driving with the radio off. We can safely assume that any differences between his or her performance under the two conditions cannot stem from individual differences – because it's the same person in both conditions.

If you are still confused by this, imagine that we developed a revolutionary kind of running shoe which we suspected would improve the running performance of those who wore it. The *between subjects* design would be like giving the shoes to half of the runners in a race and comparing their finishing positions with the runners who didn't have the new shoes. The *within subjects* design would be like getting the runners to run at least once with the shoes and once without them. In the first race, it is possible that our runners with the new shoes might find themselves up against people who were simply much better than them anyway. In the latter race, however, you can see that this wouldn't matter, because we wouldn't be interested in where our runners came in *absolute* terms, but simply how well they fared in comparison with their performance without the shoes (e.g. in time taken to complete the course). That is, in the first instance it would make a great deal of difference if they found themselves running against Carl Lewis or Sebastian Coe; in the latter case it wouldn't matter at all (provided, of course, that they ran against them on both occasions).

The within subjects design, therefore, avoids the problem of *individual differences* in ability at the experimental task. In formal terms, in eliminating individual differences from our experiment, the within subjects design reduces the amount of **inherent**, **background** or **extraneous variation** that we have to cope with, i.e. variation *other than* that arising from our manipulation of the independent variable. For this reason within subjects designs are, at least in principle, to be preferred to between subjects ones.

As you have to start somewhere, therefore, a good rule of thumb when designing experiments is to start by exploring the possibility of using a within subjects design, and only turn to the alternatives when you discover obstacles that prevent the meaningful use of this design.

*Summary of Section 9.2*

1. In all experiments the effects of the independent variable on the dependent variable are assessed against a background of *inherent* or *extraneous* variation.
2. *Individual differences* in ability at the experimental task are a considerable source of such extraneous variation.
3. The within subjects design, in eliminating *individual differences*

removes a large part of this extraneous variation. It should, therefore, be used in preference to the between subjects design when there are no insurmountable obstacles to its use.

## 9.3 Within subjects designs

The within subjects design is preferable *in principle* to the between subjects design. However, this does not mean that it is without problems and difficulties of its own.

### 9.3.1 Advantages

The major advantage of the within subjects design is that it reduces the background variation against which we have to assess the impact of the independent variable upon the dependent variable. It does this by *eliminating individual differences*. There is also a practical advantage that, as students, you will probably find extremely useful – you need fewer subjects.

### 9.3.2 Disadvantages

If it eliminates one source of variation, the within subjects design unfortunately introduces another – *order* effects. When we run a within subjects design, by definition, we will obtain more than one score from our subject (see Table 9.2). In which case, of course, we will have to present our conditions one after the other. This produces problems of its own – problems which do not exist when we run a between subjects experiment.

For example, suppose we ran our stereo experiment with a within subjects design, testing all our subjects first with the radio off and then with the radio on.

> Suppose that we found that driving actually improved when the drivers had the radio on. Can you think of an alternative explanation for this finding, other than the suggestion that it was having the radio on that led to the improvement in performance?

Well, the improvement in driving performance might simply be due to the fact that the subjects in our experiment got better at the task as they became more familiar with the driving simulator. That is, they might have got better because they became more *practised*, and, because they all did the radio on condition second, this **practice effect** contributed more to performance with the radio on than to performance with the radio off. In other words, we have here a *confounding* variable arising from the *order* in which we ran the conditions. Moreover, the same argument would apply even if we'd found the opposite: that is, if we'd found that the performance of our drivers had *deteriorated* from the first condition to the second. In this case, it could simply have been that our subjects had become *bored* with the task or were simply *fatigued* and started to make more mistakes because of this.

**Order effects** are the price we pay for eliminating individual differences in a within subjects design. They come in two forms. There are those that lead to an *improvement* in the subject's performance – things like practice, increasing familiarity with the experimental task and equipment, increasing awareness of the task demands. There are those that lead to a *deterioration* in their performance – things like loss of concentration, due to fatigue or boredom. Both sorts need to be controlled for.

### 9.3.3 Controlling for order effects

The best way of controlling for order effects is by employing a technique known as **counterbalancing**.

With this technique we ensure that each condition in our experiment follows and is preceded by every other condition an equal number of times. Thus, for each subject who does one particular sequence of conditions, there are other subjects who perform the conditions in all the other possible combinations of orders. Although in the abstract this sounds horrendously complicated, generally it can be achieved comparatively easily. So, for instance, in our driving experiment, a very simple control for order effects would be to ensure that half of the subjects drove with the radio on *before* they drove with the radio off, whilst the other half drove with the radio on *after* they had driven with it off (see Table 9.3). That way, although we would not have *eliminated* order effects (our subjects might well get better or worse as they went along) we would have rendered them *unsystematic*. That is, practice, fatigue and boredom should affect the radio on condition about as much as they affect the radio off condition.

Sometimes, however, there are too many conditions to counter-

**Table 9.3** A counterbalanced, within subjects design to examine the effects of having the radio off or on upon driving performance.

| Subject Number | Radio On | Radio Off |
|---|---|---|
| s3 | 1st | 2nd |
| s2 | 1st | 2nd |
| s6 | 1st | 2nd |
| s8 | 1st | 2nd |
| s4 | 2nd | 1st |
| s5 | 2nd | 1st |
| s1 | 2nd | 1st |
| s7 | 2nd | 1st |

NOTE:
s = subject

balance. Under these circumstances there is an alternative. This is to **randomize** the order of the conditions.

For example, if we had an experiment with six conditions, this would give us 720 different orders. If we wished to counterbalance these orders, we would need a minimum of 720 subjects (one for each different sequence of the six conditions). Although there are alternatives that you might come across later on in your statistics courses (e.g. the *latin square* design) under these circumstances you will most probably find yourselves *randomizing* the orders undertaken by your subjects.

When we randomize the order of our conditions we don't actually ensure that all the conditions are followed by and preceded by every other condition an equal number of times. Instead, we plump for a second best – we trust a *random sequence* to spread the order effects more or less equally around the various conditions. So, for instance, we would anticipate that if we correctly randomized the orders in which our subjects performed in an experiment with six experimental conditions, each of the conditions should appear in each of the ordinal positions (first, second, third etc.,) just about as often as the others. And, the more subjects we have, the likelier it is that this will be the case.

This is because the critical feature of a random sequence is that the items in the sequence all have an equal chance of being selected for any of the positions in that sequence. In the case of orders, what this means is that any of the conditions can appear first, second, third etc. for any of the subjects. So, for example, in a six condition experiment, condition A has the same chance as conditions B, C, D, E, and

F, of being the first condition undertaken by subject 1. If condition C is the one actually chosen (see Appendix 3 for the details of how to go about making such choices) then conditions A, B, D, E, and F, all have an equal chance of being the second condition undertaken by subject 1. If condition D is chosen as the second condition, then conditions A, B, E, and F, all have an equal chance of being the third condition undertaken by subject 1, and so on until all the conditions have been allocated to this subject. Moreover, the same applies to subject 2, and indeed to *all* the subjects in the experiment (Table 9.4).

**Table 9.4** Randomized orders of conditions for ten subjects in a within subjects design experiment with six conditions. Each sequence of conditions has been created randomly and separately for each subject.

| Subject number | Sequence of conditions |
| --- | --- |
| s1 | C D A E F B |
| s2 | B D F A C E |
| s3 | F D B A E C |
| s4 | A C B F D E |
| s5 | F A D E B C |
| s6 | A B F C E D |
| s7 | E D B F A C |
| s8 | C D B F E A |
| s9 | D A E B F C |
| s10 | E F C D B A |

NOTE:
s = subject

*SAQ 38*
Those among you who relish a challenge might now like to go back to SAQ 27 and work out how you could control for order effects in the two within subjects designs (a and e). State what the minimum number of subjects would be for these experiments given the controls you have chosen to employ.

Both of these techniques of controlling for order effects in a within subjects design, however, have one thing in common. They are based upon the assumption that our subjects are not much more fatigued, or bored, or practised, when the radio off condition comes after the radio on condition, than they are when the radio off condition comes first. If they are, then we have what we call a significant **carry-over effect** among the conditions in our experiment. Such effects are only partially controlled for by counterbalancing and randomization.

When you suspect that the conditions of your experiment will have such a *carry-over* effect, then you should not use a within subjects design. An extreme example of such a case would be, for instance, if we were attempting to compare two different techniques of teaching a particular task. Once the subject has learned the task once, it is basically impossible to make him/her unlearn it in order to learn it once again by the different method. Similarly, if we were undertaking research into the effects of alcohol upon mood, it would be difficult to have our no-alcohol condition following immediately upon our alcohol condition, unless we had a quick acting antidote for alcohol that we could administer to our subjects. So you must watch out for treatment conditions in your experiments that tend to markedly alter the state of your subject. Such conditions will have a lingering effect and will consequently influence performance in subsequent conditions.

If these effects are only temporary, one way around them is to introduce a longer than usual time-delay between conditions (e.g. days, or even weeks). However, if the effects are more or less permanent (e.g. teaching methods) or if this strategy is not feasible (e.g. lack of time, lack of co-operation on the part of your subjects) then it would be wise to employ one of the alternative designs.

Another problem that arises with within subjects designs is the need to duplicate and *match* materials. For example, suppose we were interested in establishing whether scores on a test of reasoning are influenced by the ways in which the questions are phrased – in particular, whether the problems are couched in *abstract* terms (e.g. using algebraic expressions like 'A > I') or in *concrete* terms (e.g. by using examples drawn from everyday life to express the same relationships – things like 'Arthur is greater than Ian'). There are profound individual differences in peoples' ability to reason, so ideally we would like to run this experiment with a within subjects design. We could do this by giving subjects *both* concrete and abstract problems and comparing their performances on the two types of item. However, we would need to make sure that any differences in performance between the two conditions arose from the ways in which the problems were expressed and not from the fact that one of the sets of problems was simply easier to solve than the other. That is, we would need to *match* our materials so that they were equivalent in all respects other than the independent variable – whether they were couched in concrete or abstract terms. In this case, this is not all that difficult to do. If you imagine two sets of problems, Test A and Test B, we can give one group of subjects Test A couched in concrete terms and Test B couched in abstract terms, and the other group of subjects Test A couched in abstract terms and Test B couched in concrete terms (Table 9.5). Thus, any differences that we find in overall performance on the concrete and abstract items can't be due to differences in the ease of the items themselves – because the two sets of items have appeared equally as often under the concrete and the abstract conditions.

**Table 9.5** A within subjects design with matched materials to examine the effects of the phrasing of the questions (concrete versus abstract) on reasoning performance.

|         | Test A   | Test B   |
|---------|----------|----------|
| Group 1 | Concrete | Abstract |
| Group 2 | Abstract | Concrete |

*Summary of Section 9.3*

1. The cost of eliminating individual differences in the within subjects design is the introduction of another source of *extraneous variation – order effects*.
2. Order effects are of two kinds: those that lead to an *improvement* and those that lead to a *deterioration* in the subject's performance on the experimental task.
3. These order effects must be *controlled* for – either by *counterbalancing* or by *randomizing* the order of the conditions.
4. These methods do not *eliminate* the variation introduced by order. They simply *transform* it into unsystematic variation.
5. These methods will not work when we have *significant* carry-over effects. Under these circumstances, within subjects designs must not be used.
6. Finally, with within subjects designs we often need to duplicate and *match* our materials.

## 9.4 Principal alternatives to the within subjects design

Where there are insurmountable order effects, or it is difficult to match materials, or when the subjects simply *have* to be different (e.g. in personality research, experiments involving differences in intelligence, race, gender etc.,) then the within subjects design is not suitable. Under these circumstances, you should turn to one of the alternatives: the between, matched-subjects, or, if you have more than one independent variable, mixed designs.

## 9.5   Between subjects designs

Where you have only one independent variable, the principal alternative to the within subjects design is the between subjects design. As pointed out earlier, however, the biggest disadvantage of the between subjects design is the presence of *individual differences*. But there are ways in which we can attempt to minimize their impact on our experiment.

### 9.5.1   Advantages

It just so happens that the advantages of the between subjects design correspond to the weaknesses of the within subjects design. That is, there are no problems with order effects, and we don't need to duplicate and match our materials.

### 9.5.2   Disadvantages

However, the reverse is also true. If there are no problems with order effects, this is more than offset by the intrusion of individual differences. And, if we don't have problems with materials, we have to find a lot more subjects.

### 9.5.3   Ways around these disadvantages

With respect to the bigger disadvantage, individual differences, we must attempt to rule out any *systematic bias* stemming from such differences between subjects. While we cannot eliminate individual differences we can try to ensure that they are equally distributed across conditions, e.g. that as many good drivers are allocated to the radio on and radio off groups. One possibility would be to try and *match* our subjects, assessing them on driving performance and making sure that equal numbers of good and bad drivers are allocated to each group. In order to do this we would need to assess the performances of our subjects *prior* to running the experiment.

Often, however, we have neither the resources nor the time to collect and act upon this information. Under these circumstances, the alternative we turn to is again *randomization* – in this instance the *random allocation* of subjects to their conditions (see Appendix 3). In this case we simply go to our pool of subjects and allocate them randomly to conditions, trusting the random sequence to spread individuals who differ in basic ability at the experimental task more or less equally among the conditions. So, for instance, in our stereo and driving experiment we might allocate our subjects to either the radio on or the radio off condition using **random number tables** (Appendix 3) or by spinning a coin so that those who obtained heads ended up in the radio on condition, those who obtained tails in the radio off condition. If the coin was fair, we would probably be happy to assume that this procedure would give us a fairly even split of good, poor, and indifferent drivers between the conditions. You can see, therefore, that the more subjects we use, the more effective this procedure is like to be.

Random *allocation* of subjects to conditions, however, is not to be confused with the random *selection* of subjects from a population. Ideally you should do both. In practice, whilst you are students, you will probably only do the former. Moreover, unless you check, you can never really be sure that your randomization has been effective. That is, you will be unable to state categorically that differences in ability among your subjects did *not* lead to the differences you observed on your dependent variable. And the same thing is true of randomizing to control for order effects. However remote, it may be that there were systematic differences in the orders in which your conditions appeared, even though these were randomized. So, if you elect not to check these possibilities, then you should bear them in mind when you come to interpret your findings.

With regard to the problem of having to obtain larger numbers of subjects with a between subjects design than with the within subjects equivalent, like the problems with materials in within subjects designs, it is simply something we have to live with. However, where you have more than one independent variable you may be able to reduce the number of these that require different subjects (i.e. employ what we call a *mixed* design), and reduce thereby the number of subjects you need overall.

*Summary of Sections 9.4–9.5*

1. The *between* subjects design *eliminates* order effects and the need to duplicate materials.
2. It *introduces* individual differences and requires larger numbers of subjects than the equivalent within subject design.
3. We can attempt to control for individual differences by allocating our subjects to conditions randomly.
4. This does not *eliminate* the variation introduced by individual differences; it is simply an attempt to render them *unsystematic*.
5. As with controlling for order effects by randomization, it is possible that allocating our subjects randomly to conditions does not completely transform the systematic variation. This should be borne in mind when findings are interpreted.

### 9.6 The matched subjects design

If you have the time and the resources to collect the relevant information, then the **matched subjects** design is a good half-way house between the between and within subjects designs. In this case what you attempt to do is to *match* your subjects so that individual differences in ability are more or less equally distributed across conditions. So, with our stereo and driving experiment, for instance, we might assess each subject's driving ability *before* allocating them to experimental conditions and then attempt to make sure that equal numbers of good and poor drivers were allocated to each group. Similarly, we might attempt to get around the problems with matching materials in our reasoning experiment by running this as a matched subjects design with equal numbers of good, poor, and indifferent reasoners in the concrete and abstract conditions. This way we don't trust to a random sequence to spread individual differences equally between conditions – we attempt to ensure that this is done ourselves.

Where possible, therefore, it is a good idea to match the subjects in an experiment in which you have different subjects in conditions, as this will reduce the possibility of individual differences *confounding* the effects of your independent variable.

However, you will of course still have to allocate the matched subjects to the experimental conditions *randomly*. That is, which particular condition any one of the better drivers or any one of the less able drivers is to go in must be decided at random in exactly the same way as you would do with a sample of non-matched subjects.

*SAQ 39*
Why?


Where you have *matched* subjects, therefore, you will still need to allocate them to experimental conditions randomly. You do this by turning to each group of matched subjects separately. So, for instance, you might start with your sample of *better* drivers and allocate them to their conditions using the sort of methods described in Appendix 3. Once all these had been allocated to their conditions (ensuring an equal number appear in each condition) you might then turn to the *less* able drivers and repeat the process. This way you would end up with the same spread of ability in each condition, but within any level of ability, subjects allocated randomly to their conditions.

One controversial aspect of this design is that it is sometimes argued that it can be treated as a *within* subjects design for the purposes of statistical analysis. As a student, however, it is extremely unlikely that in human work you will achieve the necessary level of matching for this, so you should consider the *matched subjects* design to be a *between* subjects one when analysing it.


*Summary of Section 9.6*

1. A good half-way house between the within and the between subjects design is to use a between subjects design in which the subjects have been matched and allocated to conditions such that there is an equal spread of ability on the experimental task between the conditions.
2. This is known as the *matched subjects design*, and it reduces the possibility of individual differences *confounding* the effects of the Independent Variable.


### 9.7 Experimental designs with more than one independent variable

So far we have talked exclusively about experiments with only one independent variable. However, it is perfectly possible to manipulate more than one independent variable in an experiment. Indeed, nowadays designs in which this happens are quite common in psychology.

Rather than simply concerning ourselves with the effects of having the radio on or off on driving performance, for instance, we might want to find out whether this affects those who have been drinking alcohol more than those who have not been drinking alcohol. In order to do this we could design an experiment in which we manipulated *both* the IV radio on/off, *and* the IV drinking alcohol/not drinking alcohol. How would we do this? Well, we could turn to our pool of subjects and allocate half of them randomly to a radio on condition, and half to a radio off condition. Of those in the radio on condition, we could allocate half randomly to drink a standard amount of alcohol, with the remainder remaining sober. Likewise with the radio off condition, we could ask half of our subjects to drink the standard amount of alcohol, with the other half remaining sober (Table 9.6). We would thus have manipulated *two* independent variables, (radio listening and alcohol intake) with two **levels** on each of them (radio on/radio off and alcohol intake/no alcohol intake).

**Table 9.6**    An experimental design with two factors, two levels on each factor.

| | FACTOR 1: Radio | |
| --- | --- | --- |
| | LEVEL 1 | LEVEL 2 |
| | On | Off |
| LEVEL 1: Yes | Condition 1 | Condition 2 |
| LEVEL 2: No | Condition 3 | Condition 4 |
| FACTOR 2 | | |
| Alcohol | | |

Again, we need not restrict ourselves to manipulating the *presence* versus the *absence* of the suspected causal variables. We could, for instance, vary the *amount* of alcohol our subjects consumed, so that one group drank no alcohol, another the equivalent of one glass of wine, another the equivalent of two glasses of wine, and another the equivalent of three glasses of wine. At the same time we would have half of the subjects driving with the radio on, the other half with the radio off. Such a design appears in Table 9.7. On the other hand, we could simultaneously vary the *volume* at which the radio was played – with one group listening to the radio at low volume, another at medium volume, and a third at high volume. Such a design appears in Table 9.8.

In principle, there is no limit to the number of independent variables that you can manipulate simultaneously in an experiment.

**Table 9.7** An experimental design with 2 factors, one with 2 levels, the other with 4 levels.

| | FACTOR 1: Radio | |
|---|---|---|
| | LEVEL 1 | LEVEL 2 |
| | On | Off |
| LEVEL 1: None | Condition 1 | Condition 2 |
| LEVEL 2: 1 glass wine | Condition 3 | Condition 4 |
| LEVEL 3: 2 glass wine | Condition 5 | Condition 6 |
| LEVEL 4: 3 glass wine | Condition 7 | Condition 8 |
| FACTOR 2 | | |
| Alcohol | | |

**Table 9.8** An experimental design with 2 factors, 4 levels on each factor.

| | FACTOR 1: Radio | | | |
|---|---|---|---|---|
| | LEVEL 1 | LEVEL 2 | LEVEL 3 | LEVEL 4 |
| | High Volume | Medium Volume | Low Volume | Off |
| LEVEL 1: None | Cond 1 | Cond 2 | Cond 3 | Cond 4 |
| LEVEL 2: 1 glass wine | Cond 5 | Cond 6 | Cond 7 | Cond 8 |
| LEVEL 3: 2 glass wine | Cond 9 | Cond 10 | Cond 11 | Cond 12 |
| LEVEL 4: 3 glass wine | Cond 13 | Cond 14 | Cond 15 | Cond 16 |
| FACTOR 2 | | | | |
| Alcohol | | | | |

NOTE: Cond = Condition

Neither is there any restriction over whether these variables are *between* or *within* subjects. For example, in the first version of the above experiment the variables could *both* be between subjects (with different subjects in conditions 1–4) or *both* within subjects (with the same subjects in conditions 1–4, albeit with a suitable time-lag between the alcohol and the no-alcohol conditions). We could even have a *combination* of between and within subjects variables (for instance, the variable radio on/off could be *within* subjects, the variable alcohol/no alcohol *between* subjects).

Designs such as these are known by a combination of the *number* and *nature* of their independent variables. So, for instance, the above experiment would be called a 'two factor' experiment. (In advanced circles, IV's are more usually referred to as **factors**.) If all of these factors (IV's) were between subjects, then it would be called a 'two factor, between subjects design'. If all of these factors were within subjects, it would be called a 'two factor, within subjects design'. If at least one of these factors were between subjects and at least one were within subjects, then it would be referred to as a 'two factor, **mixed** design'.

*SAQ 40*
Below you will find a list of experiments that have more than one IV. Go through each in turn and attempt to name these designs using the conventions outlined above. (Hint: first *count* the number of IV's, then work out whether each IV is between or within subjects.)

a.  An accident researcher is interested in the effects of different levels of alcohol on driving performance. Over the course of several weeks, s/he varies the quantity of alcohol given to a group of subjects on different occasions. S/he then examines whether the impact of the alcohol varies with the person's sex and the length of time since they passed their driving test.
b.  An occupational psychologist is interested in the effects of different types of stress (e.g. heat, noise, light) and the nature of the task (demanding, undemanding) on blood pressure. S/he exposes different groups of subjects to the different types of stress, and measures the performance of all of them on both types of task.
c.  A psychologist interested in personality wishes to examine the effects of sex and Extraversion on public speaking performance.
d.  Another accident researcher is interested in the effect of listening to the car radio on driving performance. Using a driving simulator, s/he varies the driving conditions, the nature of material listened to, and the volume at which it is played, on the driving performance of a group of experienced drivers.

Note that sometimes you will find between and within subjects designs with more than one IV referred to as **factorial designs**, mixed ones as **split-plot designs**.

With such designs we can not only assess the *main effects* of a factor (e.g. the impact of drinking alcohol on driving performance), but also whether there are **interactions** between the factors in our experiment. An *interaction* between the conditions of different IV's is precisely what we described above: things like whether drivers who have been drinking alcohol are affected more by having the radio on than drivers who have not been drinking alcohol. Or even whether male drivers who have been drinking and have the radio on are affected differently from female drivers who have been drinking and have the radio on.

If you wish to know more about such designs, you will need to turn to a textbook of statistics. They are dealt with in some detail in GandD. For current purposes, however, what you really need to know is how to accurately name designs in which you employ more than one IV. But a word of caution is in order: the statistical technique that is generally used to analyse such designs – **Analysis of Variance** – is immensely flexible, and in the wrong hands can be a dangerous weapon. It allows you to combine as many IV's as you wish; often too many for comfort's sake. So, when designing experiments with more than one IV *do not go overboard*! Too many IV's (more than three, or perhaps four, at the most) will make controlling for order effects complicated and interpreting the **higher order interactions** (i.e. those between three or more factors) virtually impossible. So only use designs with more than three IV's sparingly. You have been warned!

*Summary of Section 9.7*

1. It is perfectly possible nowadays to design experiments in which we manipulate more than one IV at the same time. Such designs give us a better assessment of the *main-effects* of an IV (or *factor*) than we would have obtained had we run the experiment manipulating that IV on its own, and also enable us to assess whether there is an *interaction* between the factors (IVs) in our experiment.
2. An *interaction* occurs when the effects of one factor are different at the different *levels* of another factor.
3. Such designs are known by a combination of the *number* and *nature* of their factors (IVs). These factors can be *all* between subjects, *all* within subjects, or a combination of between and within subjects factors. In principle, there is no restriction over the number of *levels* that may be used on any given factor, nor on the number of factors that might be manipulated simultaneously in any given experiment.
4. As a general rule, however, until you have become confident in your use of such designs, you would be advised to keep the number of factors you manipulate in one experiment to a maximum of three (it is difficult to interpret interactions between three or more factors).

## 9.8   The self-esteem of your subject: design and de-brief

A concern with variables and control is not the only element of experimental design in psychology. Regard for the welfare and comfort of your subjects is as integral to good experimental practice as is the pursuit of experimental rigour and elegance. Never under-estimate the impact that being in a psychological experiment can have on your subject. We live in a competitive society and the experiment has all the trappings of a test. Those of you who have participated in a psychological experiment will probably have been struck by just how difficult it can be to shake off the feeling that somehow you are under scrutiny and have to do your best, even though you know that an experimenter's interest is rarely in particular individuals, but invari-ably in making statements about the influence of his/her IV on *groups* of people. Those of you who haven't participated in one, should try to if possible. It gives you an invaluable insight into the sorts of factors that can influence a subject's performance in an experiment.

The important thing to bear in mind is always the subject's self-respect and dignity. You have no right to put your subject through an experience that undermines their self-regard. So, think about the impact that your experiment will have on your subject when you think about designs that you might employ and issues you might address by experimenting.

As the opportunity for restoring any loss of self-esteem that might occur is quite limited during the experiment itself, you must make time available for those who want it at the end of the experiment to discuss any questions they have regarding what you have asked them to do. This is known in the trade as **de-briefing** your subject, and it is an integral part of experimenting. At this stage, answer their ques-tions informatively, honestly, and willingly, discussing the thinking behind your ideas, and the purpose of the experiment if that interests them. The only time that it might not be responsible to do this is if you have undertaken an experiment in which you have used **deception**. As this is a thorny issue in itself, we'd better address it separately.

## 9.9   Deception

Sometimes you may feel that you have to deceive your subjects about the purpose of the study (e.g. where you anticipate that knowing what the study is genuinely about might influence their behaviour). Such a procedure poses profound ethical problems for psychologists. Many people argue that deception should never be used, others that it can be justifiable under certain circumstances. I leave it to your own conscience, but it goes without saying that it should never be done lightly. Before deciding to employ deception I would suggest that you satisfy yourself on at least three counts: firstly, is this the only way you can examine this question? Secondly, is the impact of the deception on the subject likely to be minimal? Finally, is the question really worth it (i.e. will the ends justify the means)? The British Psychological Society has issued a set of **ethical guidelines** (in the *Bulletin of the British Psychological Society*, January 1977), which it may be worth your while examining.

Deception poses a number of problems for de-briefing. The obvious response – 'coming clean' – may involve telling the subject, in effect, that s/he has been hoodwinked, raise the suspicion that s/he has been made a fool of, and thereby undermine both the subject's self-respect, as well as his/her opinion of psychologists. Under these circumstances you must take the advice of your tutor on whether to tell the truth or to persist with some cover story that satisfies the subject and maintains his/her self-regard.

If you do come clean, then this poses additional problems if your subjects have been drawn from a group of people that are likely to meet each other. For those who have participated in your experiment may well tell other potential subjects about what you did to them and this, of course, will seriously undermine your cover-story. There is very little you can do about this, except by attempting to convince your subjects of the importance of staying mum. One way of achieving this is by making them feel as if they have been *collaborators* rather than guinea-pigs, in your research. Thus they may be persuaded that telling others will waste the contribution they have made themselves. But be warned – you can be sure that someone, somewhere, will spill the beans.

Of course, the best way of avoiding these problems, is by not getting into this position in the first place. So, this is another factor weighing against the use of deception.

### 9.10  Pilot-testing

Once you have designed your experiment, chosen the question you wish to examine experimentally, the IV you wish to manipulate, the DV you think will best assess this IV manipulation, decided whether you would be better off comparing the same or different subjects, prepared your materials, set up your random sequences, allocated your subjects to their groups, and standardized your instructions, you might think that you're finally ready for the off. However, a little more patience at this stage may well pay dividends later. For, rather than diving straight in and running your study, a sensible procedure to adopt here is to **pilot-test** your experiment. That is, to try it out on a few subjects first to see whether it makes sense to them, to uncover any serious flaws or problems that might have been overlooked at the design stage, to generally 'tighten up' the procedure, and, at the very least, to familiarize yourself with your role as experimenter so that you are practised and professional by the time you run your first subject in earnest.

Pilot-testing can save you a lot of wasted time and effort. It provides you with a golden opportunity to modify your design *before* you've wasted too many subjects. It is, therefore, a good habit to get into. Indeed, it will become increasingly important as you take greater responsibility for designing your own experiments. It is an essential part of a final year undergraduate project.

With a pilot-test you can assess questions such as: are the instructions comprehensible? are there any problems with the materials, or the way these are presented? A pilot-test can also reveal whether you have a potential **floor** or **ceiling** effect in your data.

For instance, thinking back to the driving and stereo experiment, we need to set our subjects a course on the driving simulator that is neither so difficult that few can do it ('floor effect'), nor so easy that more or less everyone can ('ceiling effect'). Otherwise, we will not be able to assess the effects of manipulating our IV on performance itself. However, it is often difficult to decide on the appropriate level of task difficulty in the abstract. A brief pilot-test on subjects who are representative of those who will take part in the experiment proper, however, can help with this problem.

*Summary of Sections 9.8–9.10*

1. Regard for the welfare and comfort of the subjects in your experiment is an integral part of good experimental design. You have no right to put your subjects through an experience that undermines their self-respect and dignity, and you must bear this in mind when thinking about procedures you might employ and issues you might address in experiments.

2. As well as this, you should make time available at the end of your experiment to discuss any questions your subjects have regarding what you asked them to do. You should answer their questions honestly, openly, and willingly. This is known as

*de-briefing* your subject and it is an essential feature of any well-designed experiment.

3. The use of *deception* not only raises ethical difficulties, but also poses practical problems for de-briefing. You should seek the advice of your tutor before undertaking experiments involving deception.

4. A good habit to get into is to *pilot-test* your experiment by trying it out on a few subjects *before* you start to record any data. This enables you to spot any flaws in your design and gives you the opportunity to generally 'tighten up' your procedure. Pilot-testing can save you a lot of wasted time and effort.

# 10  Statistics

So far in this guide we have talked rather glibly about *differences* between conditions, and *correlations* between variables. However, what we have really meant here is what you will come to understand as differences and correlations that are *reliable* or *significant*. For there is something special about the differences that interest us – we are not interested simply in a difference in the numbers between, say, two conditions; we are interested in those differences that have a *low probability of occurring naturally*.

Thinking back to our driving and stereo experiment, if we were to measure the performance of any given subject on the driving simulator on a number of occasions, even when this subject was fully accustomed to the apparatus we would not expect him/her to obtain an *identical* number of errors on each occasion. Similarly, we have already pointed out that one of the problems with *between subjects* designs is that there are generally profound *individual differences* between people in their basic abilities on experimental tasks. This means, of course, that even where we allocate our subjects to experimental conditions *randomly*, we would hardly expect our different groups to obtain identical mean scores on the dependent variable.

If you have any doubts about this, then try the following exercise. Try balancing a book on your head (make sure it isn't too heavy, and keep away from breakable objects)! See how long you can keep it there (a) in silence and (b) with the radio on. Do it five times under each condition. (Make sure that you set up a *random* sequence *in advance*.) Record your times, and then work out the *mean* time for balancing under both conditions. Are they identical? I bet they're not. But does this mean that having the radio on has affected your ability to balance a book on your head? (I trust that you've controlled adequately for the effects of practice and fatigue.)

The point of this is that we will more or less inevitably find differences between conditions on our DV, *even when our IV does not in fact cause changes in our DV*. So, for example, even if having the radio on had absolutely no impact whatsoever on one's ability to drive, we would still expect to find our subjects apparently driving better in one of our experimental conditions than in the other. That is, we will always have to assess the effects of our independent variable against a background of *inherent* variation.

We need, therefore, to find a way of being able to recognize a difference that *has* been influenced by our independent variable (a **'reliable' difference**) from one that has *not* been so influenced – a difference that would be there anyway. That is, we need to be able to detect the sort of difference that would occur simply if we took a group of subjects and measured their performances on repeated occasions *without* exposing them to the IV. This is why we turn to **inferential statistics**.

*Summary of Section*

1. We will invariably find that there are differences between our conditions on our dependent variable even when our independent variable does not cause changes in the dependent variable.
2. We therefore have to find some way of distinguishing a difference that has been caused by our IV (a 'reliable' difference) from one that is simply the product of chance variation.
3. We employ *inferential* statistics to assist us with this task.

### 10.1   Inferential statistics

Think back to our cheese and nightmare experiment. Imagine that we actually ran this experiment and obtained the data in Table 10.1. (There are 50 subjects in each condition.) You can see from Table 10.1 that eleven more of those in the cheese condition reported nightmares than those in the no-cheese condition. Thus, *more* people reported nightmares in the cheese condition than in the no-cheese condition. This is a difference, but as yet we don't know whether it is the sort of difference we would be likely to find anyway. The question is, if eating cheese actually has *no effect* upon the incidence of nightmares, how likely would we be to obtain a difference between our conditions of eleven?

**Table 10.1**  The number of subjects reporting nightmares in the cheese and no-cheese conditions.

|  | Cheese | No Cheese |
|---|---|---|
| Number reporting nightmares | 33 | 22 |
| Number not reporting nightmares | 17 | 28 |

To understand this, imagine that we took 100 table tennis balls, and stamped 'nightmare' on half of them, and 'no nightmare' on the remainder. We then placed these in a large black plastic bag, shook them up, and drew them out one by one. Imagine also that we simply decided to allocate the first fifty table tennis balls we drew out to a hypothetical 'cheese' condition, and the remainder to a hypothetical 'no cheese' condition. The question is, doing this, how likely would we be to get the sorts of scores that we have in Table 10.1?

Ideally we need some way of assessing this. And this is precisely where *inferential* statistics come in. These statistics enable us to assess the likelihood that we would obtain our results if our independent variable did *not* cause changes in our dependent variable. Using such statistics we can assess whether we would have been likely to get data like ours if there really wasn't any genuine effect of eating cheese on the incidence of nightmares – in this instance, the probability that we would obtain scores like those in Table 10.1 if we actually *did* draw suitably labelled table tennis balls from our big black plastic bag.

There are various techniques available to enable us to assess this likelihood for data obtained under all sorts of circumstances. (Advice on how to go about choosing an appropriate test can be found in section 10.3.) For all of these, however, at the end of the calculations you should end up with a single score (the *statistic*). This is the value that 'belongs' to your data. By looking this up in the appropriate table we can find out how likely we would be to obtain this value – and by implication, these data – by chance alone. For instance, the appropriate statistic for the above example is **chi-square**. Chi-square actually tests for an *association* between two variables – in this case whether there is any association between eating cheese and the numbers of nightmares that are reported. So, you can see that it is eminently suited for the question we wish to ask of our data.

You will find details of how to calculate chi-square in almost any textbook of statistics. It is in GandD. Using the appropriate formula, we can calculate the value of chi-square that belongs to the data in Table 10.1. In this case the value is $\chi^2 = 4.4$. What we need to do now is to find out whether this value is *likely* or *unlikely* to have occurred anyway, without our manipulation of the independent variable. In practice, we do this by looking up a table of **critical values** for the statistic in question – in this case, chi-square. There we find a list of values of chi-square, together with their likelihood of occurring naturally. By comparing our *obtained* value of chi-square (4.4) with the **tabled** or *critical* values, we can find out whether our data was likely or unlikely to have occurred anyway. For instance, in Table 10.2, you can see that a value of $\chi^2 = 0.15$ has a probability of occurring of p=0.7 which is quite high. A value of $\chi^2 = 3.84$ however, has an associated probability of only p=0.05 which is quite low.

**Table 10.2**  Probabilities associated with particular values of Chi-square with one degree of freedom.

| Chi-square | Probability |
|---|---|
| 0.016 | 0.9 |
| 0.15 | 0.7 |
| 0.46 | 0.5 |
| 1.64 | 0.2 |
| 3.84 | 0.05 |
| 5.02 | 0.025 |
| 10.83 | 0.001 |

For those new to the idea of **probability**, it is measured conventionally from One to Zero. An event with a probability of 1 is *inevitable*. An event with a probability of 0 is *impossible*. Most events in our universe lie somewhere between these two extremes.

In order to look up the correct value of chi-square, however, we need one other piece of information – in this case the number of *degrees of freedom* associated with our data.

**Degrees of freedom** is a statistical concept that you will find explained in GandD. Basically, it is derived from the number of scores that are fed into the statistic's formula. In Table 4.3 you will see that you need to know this value for most of the tests that you are likely to use. Fortunately – as it is rather a difficult concept to grasp –

you need actually lose little sleep over it. For you can derive the appropriate degrees of freedom for most tests simply by calculation (in all tests the appropriate formula will be provided). In the case of data like ours, the degrees of freedom are derived from the numbers of rows and columns we have in our table of data, and are given by the formula:

(No. of Rows – 1) × (No. of Columns – 1)

*SAQ 41*
In this case, therefore, where we have 2 rows and 2 columns, what is the value of our degrees of freedom?

We therefore need to look up the probability associated with our obtained value of chi-square with one degree of freedom. (You will find **tables of critical values** in most textbooks of statistics, including GandD.) On looking this up, we find that a value of $\chi^2 = 4.4$, with 1 df, has a probability of occurring by chance of somewhere between $p=0.05$ and $p=0.025$. For, the value of chi-square that has a probability of $p=0.05$, is 3.84, which is *less* than our obtained value. But the value of chi-square that has a probability of $p=0.025$, is 5.02, which is *greater* than our obtained value. So, our value lies somewhere in between these, and consequently the probability associated with it must lie somewhere between $p=0.05$ and $p=0.025$.

The probability of obtaining a value of chi-square as *large* as 4.4 simply by chance, therefore, is somewhere between 5 and 2.5 times in a 100 (this is just another way of expressing 0.05 and 0.025). Essentially, therefore, if we were to draw our table tennis balls randomly from our big black plastic bag we would expect, *on average*, to obtain data like ours somewhere between 5 and 2.5 times for every 100 times we did it.

*SAQ 42*
Our obtained value of chi-square lies below $p=0.05$. Is this nearer the inevitable or the impossible end of the continuum? (i.e. is this nearer 1 or 0?).

Let's recap. We've run our experiment and generated the data in Table 10.1. We then realized that in order to make any sense of it – in order to find out what it tells us about the relationship between eating cheese and experiencing nightmares – we needed to discover how likely we would have been to obtain results like these anyway (i.e. if cheese had absolutely no effect whatsoever upon the incidence of nightmares). So, we employed the statistical technique appropriate for the question we wished to address (in this case, chi-square) and we discovered that the value of chi-square we obtained (4.4) has a low probability of having occurred by chance. Does this mean, therefore, that we can safely conclude that eating cheese induces nightmares?

Well, the simple and rather unsettling answer to that question is – no. For the problem is that we still don't know whether the results occurred by chance. All we know is that the probability that they did so is *low*. It is *unlikely* that they did, but still *possible*. We know therefore that we would be unlikely to draw a similar distribution of scores to those in Table 10.1 from our big black plastic bag of table tennis balls but, on any given occasion, we might actually do so. We have, in fact, somewhere between a 20–1 and a 40–1 chance of doing so. And, as some of us know to our occasional benefit, long-shots, though infrequently, still win races.

In fact we will *never* know whether our results occurred by chance. We can only ever know the probability that they *might* have done. Inferential statistics don't provide us with sudden insights into the laws of the universe. They simply tell us the probability that the scores we have obtained on our dependent variable have of having occurred by chance.

So how do we get around this problem? Well, all is not lost. What we do is set up a criterion probability for our statistic and decide that if the *probability* associated with our obtained statistic falls *above* this criterion (i.e. is nearer 1) then we will assume that the results had indeed occurred by chance, whereas, if it falls *at* or *below* this criterion (i.e. is the same value as the criterion *probability*, or nearer zero) then we will assume that the results had not occurred by chance. You can see this depicted in Figure 10.1.

This is the principle of *statistical inference*. We always do this when we test our data for differences between conditions. The criterion is referred to as the **significance level**. Although we are free to vary it, conventionally it is set at a probability of less than or equal to 0.05 (in other words 20–1, or 5 times in a 100). This is known as the **five per cent significance level** (Figure 10.2).

What we do, therefore, is compare the probability associated with our **obtained statistic** with our significance level. If our obtained statistic has a probability *greater* than our significance level (i.e. nearer 1, a more probable event) then we decide to act as if we had no evidence to reject the assumption that our results occurred by chance. Findings such as these we call statistically **non-significant**. If, however, the probability associated with our obtained statistic *equals* or is *less* than the significance level (i.e. nearer zero, a less probable event) then we decide to act as if we had sufficient evidence to *reject* the assumption that our results occurred by chance. Such data we call statistically **significant**. Under these circumstances we would talk of a 'significant difference' between our conditions. (Figure 10.2).

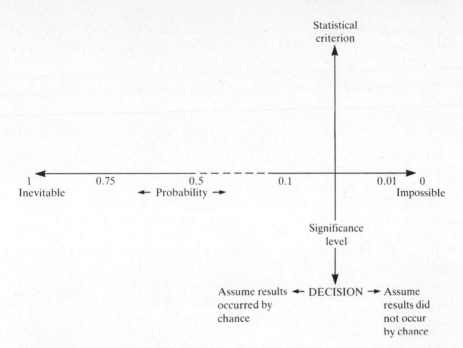

**Figure 10.1** Statistical Inference
If the probability associated with the obtained statistic falls to the left of the statistical criterion (i.e. nearer p=1), assume the results occurred by chance. If it falls to the right (i.e. nearer p=0), then assume that the results did not occur by chance.

This terminology, though widely used, is nevertheless unfortunate. To call our results non-significant does not under any circumstances mean that they are necessarily *psychologically* in-significant. Likewise, calling our results *significant*, does not necessarily mean that they have much *psychological* importance. This is a common confusion. Significance, in this context, is a *statistical* concept. It merely tells us something about the statistical nature of our data. The *psychological* importance of a set of findings, whether significant or not, remains to be established.

Moreover, when we talk about *deciding* whether or not to assume that our results occurred by chance, we rather flatter ourselves. In practice you should not think of this as a decision that you are at liberty to make – it is one that you are *compelled* to make by the outcome of your analysis. *If* the probability associated with your *obtained* statistic turns out to be *equal to or less than* the significance level then, according to the conventions governing this procedure, you have no option but to assume that your results have not occurred by chance. If, however, the probability associated with your obtained

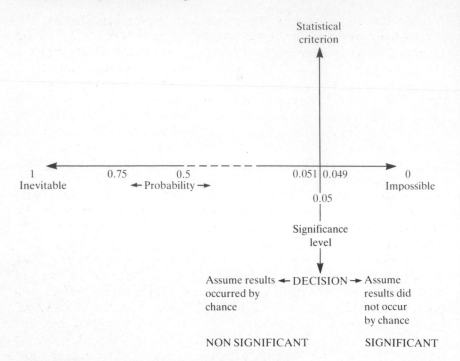

**Figure 10.2** The five per cent significance level
If the probability associated with the obtained statistic is greater than
p=0.05, assume the results occurred by chance. If this probability is equal to
or less than p=0.05, then assume that the results did not occur by chance.

statistic turns out to be *greater* than the significance level (if only by a
minute amount) then you have no option but to assume that your
results have occurred by chance.

In the case of our cheese and nightmare experiment, we calculated
a value of chi-square = 4.4. We need now to find out whether this is
*significant* at the five per cent level. This means that we need to
discover whether the probability associated with $\chi^2=4.4$ is less than or
equal to p=0.05. Earlier we established that the probability associated with $\chi^2=4.4$ with 1 degree of freedom lay somewhere between
p=0.05 and p=0.025.

*SAQ 43*
Is our value of $\chi^2$, therefore, significant at the 5 per cent significance level?

You may have noticed something interesting here. The value of $\chi^2$
with a probability equal to 0.05 and with one degree of freedom is
$\chi^2=3.84$, which is *less* than our obtained value. Yet we have decided
to call our results *significant*. If this strikes you as contradictory, then

you are the victim of a simple confusion. We decide whether our results are significant or not by comparing our *obtained* value of the statistic (the one we *calculate*) with the *critical* value (the one we look up in the table). In some tests (e.g. chi-square) in order to be significant the obtained value must be *equal to or greater than* the critical value. In other tests (e.g. the Mann Whitney U test) the obtained value must be *equal to or less than* the critical value (see Table 4.3). Irrespective of this, however, the *probability* associated with a significant value of the statistic will *always* be *less than or equal to* the *probability* of the critical value. That is, there are two separate components here – the *value* of the obtained statistic (which in some tests of significance needs to be greater than or equal to the critical value for significance) and the *probability* associated with the obtained value (which, for significance, must always be less than or equal to the significance level).

The assumption that our results occurred by chance you have met before. It is called the *null hypothesis*. In effect, therefore, at the end of our experiment, having analysed our data, we find ourselves in a position to make a decision regarding the null hypothesis – that is, whether to **accept** or to **reject** it. And we do this on the basis of whether or not the probability associated with our obtained statistic is less than or equal to the significance level we set prior to running our experiment.

*Summary of Section 10.1*

1. *Inferential* statistics tell us how likely we would be to have obtained our data simply by chance – if our independent variable did *not* cause changes in the dependent variable. They do not, however, tell us whether or not our results actually *did* occur by chance.
2. Therefore, we can never know for definite whether our results were the product of more than chance variation.
3. We get some way around this problem by adopting a criterion probability. We call this the *significance level*.
4. Although we are at liberty to alter the significance level, it is set conventionally at $p=0.05$. This is known as the 'five percent significance level'.
5. If the *probability* associated with our obtained statistic is *less than or equal to* our significance level, we act as if our results did not occur by chance. Such results we call *significant*. Effectively we decide under these circumstances to *reject* the null hypothesis.

6. If the probability associated with our obtained statistic is *greater than* our significance level, we act as if the results did occur by chance. Such results we call *non-significant*. Effectively we decide under these circumstances to *accept* the null hypothesis.

7. In practice we decide whether to accept or reject the null hypothesis by comparing our *obtained* value of the statistic with a *critical* value that we obtain from the appropriate set of statistical tables. With some tests our obtained value of the statistic has to be equal to or greater than the critical value for us to attain significance. With other tests, the obtained value of the statistic has to be equal to or less than the critical value to be significant.

8. **Significance** is a *statistical* concept.

   To say that a difference is significant or non-significant does not mean that *psychologically* the difference has much theoretical significance, or that the absence of a difference is trivial.

### 10.2   Type 1 and Type 2 errors

At the end of our experiment, therefore, we will have decided whether to accept or to reject the null hypothesis. But the simple fact is – *we could always be wrong*. That is, we may find ourselves *rejecting* the null hypothesis when – had we seen the tablets of stone on which are written the laws of the universe – we would find that the null hypothesis should, in fact, have been *accepted*. For instance, in the case of our cheese and nightmare experiment, our obtained value of chi-square is 4.4, which has an associated probability that is less than the conventional significance level of $p=0.05$. Using this significance level, therefore, we would have to reject the null hypothesis. But suppose you receive a visitation from the powers that run the universe, who reveal to you that actually the null hypothesis was in this case correct. Under these circumstances we would have *rejected* the null hypothesis when we should have *accepted* it (because it was true). This is known as a **type 1 error**. Moreover, not only is it an integral feature of the process of statistical inference – of acting as if we know something for definite when we don't – but, in this world at least, we never know whether we have made it (visitations from the powers that run the universe aside). However, we do know the *probability* that we have.

> What is the probability of making a type 1 error (i.e. of incorrectly rejecting the null hypothesis)?

The probability of incorrectly rejecting the null hypothesis is, in fact, the significance level. We decide to reject the null hypothesis when the probability associated with our obtained statistic reaches the significance level. Under these circumstances we *always* reject the null hypothesis, even though sometimes such unlikely results do occur by chance. In fact, with the five per cent significance level, there is a 20–1 chance that our results have indeed occurred by chance. Which means that, because we reject the null hypothesis *every* time our data reaches this level, we will make a mistake, on average, once every twenty times we do it.

So, what can we do about this? After all, we would like to minimize our mistakes. We don't want *too* many of the factual assertions we make about the psychological universe to be wrong. Well, if our significance level is a measure of our type 1 error rate, then one thing we might do is to reduce it – i.e. to *make our significance level more stringent* (Figure 10.3). For a significance level of p=0.01 has a type 1 error rate of only 1 in 100, rather than the 5 in 100 (or 1 in 20) of the p=0.05 significance level.

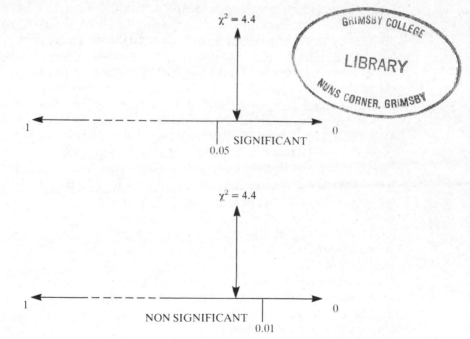

**Figure 10.3** The effects of making the significance level more stringent

Now this isn't necessarily wrong. But a number of things should be borne in mind here. Firstly, although we can get the probability of making a type 1 error *closer* to zero, the only way we can actually *make* it zero is by saying nothing at all about the existence or non-existence of a reliable difference between the conditions in our experiment. If we wish to say anything at all, therefore, we will have to accept some probability of making a type 1 error.

In fact making the significance level more stringent is a very *conservative* thing to do. Sometimes it may be the appropriate step to take (e.g. those who undertake research into ESP tend to employ more stringent criteria in the hope of persuading others of the sheer improbability that their results have occurred by chance). However, our job as scientists is essentially to make the best guesses we can about the existence of causal relationships. Making the significance level more stringent may well reduce our tendency to make mistakes, but it does so at the cost of reducing our ability to say anything. Take it too far and we are in danger of throwing the scientific baby out with the statistical bathwater.

To put it another way. In making the significance level more stringent, we are indeed reducing the probability of making a *type 1 error* – of rejecting a null hypothesis that should have been accepted. But, at the same time, we are *increasing* the probability of making another type of error – that is, of *accepting* the null hypothesis, when we should really have *rejected* it. This is known as a **type 2 error**.

For instance, suppose that we had adopted the p=0.01 level of significance for our cheese and nightmare experiment. With $\chi^2 = 4.4$ (our obtained value) we would not have achieved significance, and so would have been compelled to accept the null hypothesis (Figure 10.3). But, suppose on the tablets of stone that contain the laws of the universe was written that eating cheese will induce nightmares in humans. By making our criterion too stringent, we would therefore have missed the opportunity to make a correct statement about the universe in which we live.


*Summary of Section 10.2*

1. Sometimes we will *reject* the null hypothesis when it was in fact true. This is known as a *type 1 error*. We cannot avoid making such errors if we wish to say anything positive about the psychological universe.
2. The probability of making a *type 1 error* is the *significance level*. We can, therefore, reduce the likelihood of making a type 1 error by reducing the significance level. However, this *increases* the probability of making a *type 2 error* – of *accepting* the null hypothesis when it was in fact wrong.

3. The conventional significance levels (p=0.05 and p=0.01) are compromises between the rates for these two types of error.

### 10.3 Choosing a statistical test

This, then, is the procedure in principle. It is the same for all tests of significance. However, how you realize this procedure in practice depends on the precise *test* you need to employ to analyse your data. For you will have to employ different tests of significance under different circumstances if you wish to arrive at a meaningful answer to the same question: must I accept or reject the null hypothesis in my experiment?

Choosing the appropriate statistical test is the key to the whole process of finding out exactly what your data has to tell you. But it is nowhere near as daunting a process as most of you seem to believe. If you keep a clear head and take things *step by step*, most of the time you should have few problems in arriving at an appropriate test of your data. Indeed, your problems will be reduced in this respect if you do what most of you are told, and few of you take notice of – think about how you are going to analyse your data *before* you start running your study and *modify* the design if you forsee any problems.

In order to decide which test to employ, you need to be able to answer a number of questions about the *type of study* you conducted, the *nature of the data* you obtained, and the *precise questions you wish to ask* of these data. Below is a list of the major questions you should consider:

1. Do you want to (a) *compare conditions* or (b) *correlate variables*?
2. What type of *data* do you have? Are they (a) *nominal* (b) *ordinal* or (c) at least *interval*?
3. If at least *interval*, are your scores *normally distributed*?
4. If you wish to *compare conditions*, did you manipulate more than one IV in your study?
5. If you wish to *compare conditions*, how many do you wish to compare *at any one time*?
6. Did you have the *same* or *different* subjects in these conditions?

We haven't the space here to deal in any great detail with the concepts underlined above. They should be discussed in any reasonable textbook of statistics, and are covered well in GandD.

Essentially, the answer to question one will govern whether you employ a test of differences (a) or a correlation (b) (see Chapter 8).

The answer to question two, in turn, will help you to decide whether a **parametric** or **non-parametric test** is more appropriate. You can use the former if the answer to question two is *interval*, the answer to question three is *yes*, and certain other conditions are satisfied (see GandD).

Essentially the difference between these two families of tests (parametric and non-parametric) is that your data has to meet more stringent requirements, including the assumption that the scores in the hypothetical population from which your data has been sampled are *normally distributed*, if you wish to employ a *parametric* test. The benefit of meeting these demands – of building this extra rigour into your experiment – is the availability of a whole range of tests that are generally more flexible and powerful than their *non-parametric* equivalents.

Another requirement of the parametric test is that your data should have been measured on an *interval* scale. Data is **interval** when you have measured your dependent variable on a scale that enables you to assume that the gap between any two adjacent scores is always the same. For instance, we know that the gap between ten degrees and twenty degrees Celsius is the same as the gap between fifty and sixty degrees Celsius. The difference in temperatures is the same wherever we take temperatures that are ten degrees Celsius apart.

However, is the gap between an IQ of 105 and one of 115 the same as the gap between IQ 145 and IQ 155? That is, does a gap of ten IQ points measure the same amount of intelligence wherever it occurs? If not, then IQ scores are not measured on an *interval* scale. Indeed, it seems that many of the scales used in psychological measurement do *not* have equal intervals between adjacent points.

Where we are unable to assume equal intervals between points on the scale, we can often at least *rank order* the numbers. That is, we can say that an IQ of 155 is *greater* than one of 145, and *less* than one of 165, even if we can't assume that it is equidistant between them. When the most that we can do is this, we call our data **ordinal**.

There are occasions, however, when we cannot even rank order our data. When this occurs – when we simply have *categories* composed solely of *frequencies*, then our data is **nominal**. For example, in our cheese and nightmare experiment our data simply fell into the categories 'nightmare' or 'no nightmare'. We have no idea whether those in the experimental condition experienced nightmares that were *more* nightmarish than those in the control condition. All we can say about any given subject was whether they fell into the category 'nightmare' or 'no nightmare'. Such data – counts of individuals who fall into particular categories – is *nominal*.

The answers to questions four, five, and six will control the precise test you choose. For instance, if you are satisfied that your data fulfills the requirements for a *parametric* test, and you have manipulated more than one IV, then you will probably look for the appropriate *Analysis of Variance* to perform. On the other hand, if you only wish to compare two conditions on one IV, you are not happy to make the assumptions necessary for the parametric test, and you are comparing data from the *same* subjects, then you might consider using the *Wilcoxon signed-ranks* test.

You can see from question six above that the type of test you use will depend to some extent on whether or not you are making comparisons *between* or *within* subjects. Thus the issues we discussed in Chapter 9 directly affect the type of statistical operations you are to perform on the data. However, there is one potential source of confusion here – whether or not you should consider the *matched-subjects* design to be a between or a within subjects design for the purposes of analysis.

The matching of subjects across the different conditions in your experiment, if done properly, can considerably reduce the confounding impact of individual differences. Indeed, sometimes subjects in experiments are actually paired off and direct comparisons are made between the scores of the two subjects in a pair who are subjected to the different experimental treatments. Under these circumstances the matched-subjects design becomes the **matched-pairs design**. When this level of matching is achieved some authors argue that you can treat the scores from any pair of subjects as if they were scores from the *same* subject and analyse the data using *within* subjects techniques. (There are considerable statistical advantages to this.) However, as a student you are extremely unlikely to be involved in an experiment which involves matching subjects at the level necessary to enable you to do this. So, for your purposes, where you have *different* subjects in your conditions (even when matched) you should analyse this using the appropriate *between* subjects analysis.

You can see from this discussion that your choice of test depends heavily on the answers to the questions posed at the beginning of this section. So you will need to familiarize yourself with the concepts denoted above. Once you have done this, you might like to try your hand at the following SAQ:

*SAQ 44*
The studies below are those outlined in SAQ 27. For full details, see SAQ 27. Go through each in turn, assessing for each the answer to the above questions and arriving at a recommendation for a suitable statistical test.
How might we find out whether there was any effect:
1. of word frequency on time taken to decide whether a stimulus was a word or a non-word (in millisecs.)?

2. of oestrogen on body-weight (in grammes)?
3. of the level of anxiety on the number of viewers who took up the opportunity to make dental appointments?
4. of the nature of television violence on the mean level of shock (in volts) administered by the viewers of the violence?
5. of working with others on the number of packets of breakfast cereal packed in 20 minutes?

One common source of confusion here stems from the feeling that there should be one *best* way of analysing a given set of data. However, it is not at all unusual to find that there may be more than one way of meaningfully analysing a given set of data. For instance, even where your data fully satisfy the requirements of *parametric* tests, it is still perfectly permissible to analyse them with an appropriate *non-parametric* test. (The reverse, however, is certainly *not* true – that is, there are data that can *only* be analysed non-parametrically.) Moreover, under these circumstances you might even find that you reach a *different* decision over whether to accept or reject the null hypothesis. This is because parametric tests are generally more *powerful* than their non-parametric equivalents, and power in this sense refers to the probability of correctly rejecting the null hypothesis (i.e. of rejecting the null hypothesis when it is indeed false.)

For the purposes of your report, however, you must never *duplicate* tests in this way. That is, under these circumstances you should choose to perform and report only *one* of the relevant tests.

*Summary of Section 10.3*

1. Choosing the appropriate statistical test is the key to the whole process of arriving at a meaningful answer to the question: must I *accept* or *reject* the null hypothesis in my experiment?
2. In order to decide which test to employ, you will need to familiarize yourself with the differences between *parametric* and *non-parametric* tests of significance, and with the different *types of data* that you might gather.
3. Often there may be more than one way of meaningfully analysing a given set of data. Under these circumstances, however, you should report the outcome of only *one* of the tests available to you.

## 10.4  2-tailed and 1-tailed tests of significance

One final point concerns the question of whether to use a **2-tailed** or a **1-tailed test of significance**. This relates to whether or not you consider your experimental hypothesis to be bi-directional or uni-directional, and it introduces us to yet another controversy.

Earlier we argued that you should consider your experimental hypothesis to be uni-directional if you were able (for sound theoretical reasons) to specify the *direction* in which the difference between your conditions should occur. Some authors argue that this translates directly into whether or not you should employ a one or a two tailed test of significance.

The difference between a one and a two tailed test of significance has to do with the way in which you use the tails of the distributions of whatever statistic you are employing. (If you want to know precisely what it involves you will need to turn to your textbook of statistics.) What it means in practice is that you can obtain significance with data using a 1-tailed test that would fail to reach significance with a 2-tailed test. This is your reward for specifying the direction in which the postulated difference will occur.

Now, you may read elsewhere that whether or not you choose to employ a 1-tailed or a 2-tailed test depends on whether your experimental hypothesis is uni- or bi-directional. That is, on whether or not you have reasonable grounds for specifying in advance (*a priori*) that one of your conditions will exceed another on your DV. Unfortunately, however, it is not quite as simple as that.

It is recommended here that you employ the 1-tailed test *only* when you have asked a 'whether or not' question of your data. That is, a question of the form, 'whether or not' a particular teaching method improves the rate at which people learn a particular task, or 'whether or not' a particular set of work conditions improves output. Under these circumstances if you find a difference between your conditions that is opposite to the one you hypothesized (for example, that the teaching method actually *impairs* the rate at which people learn the task, or the work conditions actually *decrease* output) this would mean the same to you as if you had found *no-difference* between your conditions (that the new teaching method was no quicker than the old one, or that production was similar under the usual working conditions).

In practice, such questions generally concern those faced with an *applied* problem. As students, however, most of the time you will be asking questions in which findings that *contradict* predictions based on the theories that originally provoked the experiments will be every bit as important as findings that are *consistent* with these predictions, even though you were able to specify in advance the *direction* in which the difference should go. So, most of the time you will be as interested in findings that go in the opposite direction to the one you specified, and your test should therefore be two-tailed. Only when your experimental question can simply be either confirmed or refuted – when it is open to a simple yes or no answer – should you employ the one-tailed test of significance.

Most tables of statistics contain the probability values for 2-tailed comparisons. Deriving the 1-tailed value is quite simple, however. You simply halve the significance level. So, if the value you obtain is significant at the 5 per cent level (2-tailed), then the significance for a 1-tailed test is actually 2.5 per cent.

*SAQ 45*
The value of t=6.31 is the critical value of t with one degree of freedom at the 5 per cent significance level for a 1-tailed test. What is its associated probability for a 2-tailed test?

*SAQ 46*
Below are a number of results of statistical analyses. Look these up in the appropriate tables (you will find these at the rear of most decent textbooks of statistics, including GandD). For each of these state whether the result is significant at the 5 per cent level, 2-tailed.

1. The data were analysed using the Wilcoxon Signed-Ranks test (W=45, N=22). Is there evidence for any differences between conditions in the number of words recalled?
2. The data were analysed using the Mann-Whitney U test (U=8, n1=10, n2=12). Is there evidence for any differences between the treatment groups in their body weights (in grammes)?
3. The data were analysed using Chi-square ($\chi^2$=3.80, df=1). Is there any evidence for an association between eating cheese and the incidence of nightmares?
4. The data were analysed using the independent t test (t=2.2, df=16). Is there any evidence for differences between the treatment groups in their body weights (in grammes)?
5. The data were analysed using a two-way, between subjects Analysis of Variance (F=5.2, df1=2, df2=25). Is there any evidence of a main effect of volume on the time taken to complete the simulated course?

One final thing to bear in mind about your analyses is that statistics only deal with the numbers fed into them. A statistical test will churn around any set of numbers fed in in a suitable format. The delivery of a statistic at the end of this process doesn't necessarily sanctify the data. Just because your data was analysed doesn't mean either that the analysis itself or its outcome was necessarily meaningful. For instance, our value of chi-square for the cheese and nightmare experiment is perfectly reasonable, given the numbers we fed into the analysis. But this doesn't, of course, tell us anything about the relationship between eating cheese and experiencing nightmares – I made the numbers up (sorry!). And bear in mind also that rejecting the null hypothesis doesn't automatically entail that the results went in the direction you predicted. I am constantly amazed how few students actually *look* at their data once they've analysed it, or think at all deeply about what the results mean. Get into the habit of going *back* to your data and thinking about what the outcome of your analyses might mean. (This is particularly a problem where you reject the null hypothesis and yet the direction of the difference is in fact *opposite* to the one you predicted with a uni-directional hypothesis.)

*Summary of Section 10.4*

1. Tests of significance can be 1-tailed or 2-tailed. The difference in practice between these versions of the same test is that you can obtain significance with the 1-tailed version with data that would fail to reach significance using the 2-tailed version.
2. You are able to use 1-tailed tests when you are prepared to *ignore* any differences that occur in the direction *opposite* to the one predicted by your experimental hypothesis. When you will *not* ignore such differences (even though these would contradict your experimental hypothesis) your test is 2-tailed. Most of you, most of the time, will therefore be undertaking 2-tailed tests.
3. Just because your data has been analysed statistically doesn't mean that the analysis or its outcome is necessarily meaningful. You must get into the habit of going back to your data to interpret the outcomes of your analyses, and to ensure that these outcomes appear to make sense. In particular, watch out for occasions when you've been compelled to *reject* the null hypothesis and yet the differences between your conditions are in fact *opposite* in direction to the ones you predicted.

### 10.5    Summary of the statistical procedure for hypothesis testing

1. Decide whether your *inferential* question involves *comparing* conditions or *correlating* variables.
2. Choose a test that asks this question and that is appropriate for the data gathered in your study.
3. Decide what significance level you will adopt, and whether your test will be 1 or 2-tailed.
4. Calculate the *obtained* value of the above statistic.

5. Look in the appropriate set of tables for the statistic used, at the significance level you have adopted, to find the relevant *critical* value of the statistic. Depending on the test you used, you will need to know the *degrees of freedom* or the *numbers* of observations (Table 4.3) to find the correct critical value. Moreover, whether the obtained value has to be greater or less than the critical value for significance, will also depend on the test.

6. If your *obtained* value differs from the *critical* value in the direction required for significance, or if it is *equal* to the critical value, then your data is (statistically) significant. Under these circumstances, *reject* the null hypothesis.

7. If your *obtained* value differs from the *critical* value in the direction opposite to that required for significance, then your data is (statistically) non-significant. Under these circumstances, *accept* the null hypothesis.

8. Go away and think about why your data has compelled you to accept/reject the null hypothesis. What, if anything, is it telling you about the relationship between the Independent and the Dependent variables?

# Appendix 1    Why you shouldn't predict the null hypothesis

You can never design a meaningful experiment in which your theoretical arguments result in the prediction that there will be *no difference* between your conditions on the DV. This is because the logic by which we run experiments only tells us something about ideas that predict *differences* between our conditions. In order to understand this fully, we need to remind ourselves about the function that the null hypothesis serves in an experiment.

When we analyse our data statistically, what we basically do is decide how tenable the null hypothesis is. That is, we essentially suppose that there is no real effect of the IV upon the DV and then assess the likelihood that, if this were the case, we would have obtained data like ours.

Once we've analysed our data, therefore, we do one of two things. According to how low we've found the probability of obtaining our difference to be, we either *accept* or *reject* the hypothesis that the difference arose by chance. That is, we either accept or reject the *null hypothesis*. If we accept the null hypothesis, we are electing to accept the assumption that the difference could have arisen by chance. Consequently, predicting the null hypothesis can never be a test of theoretical ideas, because the null hypothesis is the outcome we'd expect if only chance factors were operating in our experiment.

For example, suppose you are interested in biological theories of personality. On reading around the area you come across two theories concerning the biological basis of Extraversion. One of these predicts that, after exposure to ultra-sound, the blood pressure of extraverts will be higher than the blood pressure of introverts. The other theory, however, predicts no such difference.

Now, for personal reasons, you favour the theory which predicts that there will be no difference in the blood pressure of the extraverts and introverts. So, you design an experiment to test this proposition. You expose extraverts and introverts to ultra-sound and measure their blood pressure. On analysing this data, you find that there is no reliable evidence for any difference in blood pressure between extraverts and introverts following exposure to ultrasound. That is, you accept the null hypothesis in your experiment.

Now you are happy with the outcome. It is evidence against the theory you disfavour. But don't be *too* happy – it is not evidence *for* the theory you favour. Although the evidence is *consistent* with what you'd expect under your favoured theory, it does not count as proof of it.

For example, suppose someone argues that babies are brought by storks who drop them down chimneys to their mothers. But suppose that you don't like this explanation. Instead you favour one that proposes that babies are brought along by the doctor or midwife in their bags. Now, we can devise a simple test of this. If babies *are* dropped down chimneys by storks, then we would expect to find mothers having babies only in houses with chimneys – not, for example, in high-rise flats, or houses with chimneys that have been blocked up. However, if they are brought by the midwife or doctor, then there should be no such difference.

So, imagine we conduct this study and find, perhaps not surprisingly, that there is no difference in the relative frequency with which babies are born to mothers in houses with chimneys and houses without chimneys. This is evidence *against* the stork theory. But, is it evidence *for* the midwife/doctor theory? Really?

The point is that such studies – such experiments – are actually only tests of the propositions that led to the expectation of a difference. They say nothing about the propositions that lead to the expectation of *no* difference. If you want to test these, then you must create a situation (i.e. design an experiment) in which your propositions predict that there will be a *difference* between your conditions. Otherwise, you will be testing the ideas you *don't* like, not the ones you *do* like.

*SAQ 47*
There's only one way in which the outcome of an experiment designed to test a proposition that predicts a difference between your conditions can tell you something about a proposition that predicts no difference between your conditions. Can you imagine when this is?

If you are confused, don't worry unduly. Just remember that *accepting* the null hypothesis at the end of your experiment only tells you something about the ideas that led to the prediction of a difference (the experimental hypothesis) and nothing about ideas that led to the prediction of no difference (the null hypothesis). If your predictions coincide with the null hypothesis, you are not actually testing your ideas.

# Appendix 2  Writing reports of questionnaire or scale based studies

For some time I have been aware that students are having difficulties fitting questionnaire or scale-based studies into the practical report. In some respects this isn't surprising – as we learnt in Chapter 1, the report as you know it is designed primarily for the reporting of experiments, so fitting survey studies into it is often akin to attempting to fit the proverbial square peg into the invariably unyielding round hole.

The major problems come with the DESIGN and PROCEDURE. For some questionnaire/scale-based studies, trying to write the DESIGN in terms of IVs, DVs, experimental hypotheses etc., is a mistake – for your study, in being non-experimental, lacks these features. However, not all questionnaire/scale-based studies are of this kind – indeed, most of the time you will be using a questionnaire/scale as an experimental tool. The problem, under these circumstances, is usually teasing out the IVs, DVs, hypotheses etc. In order to decide how to write up such studies, therefore, you have first to work out the precise use to which you put your questionnaire/scale.

Essentially, there are four main options. Firstly, you may use the questionnaire/scale to *manipulate an IV* – e.g. by presenting different material to different subjects in the context of a questionnaire. In such an instance, the different forms the questionnaire/scale takes will constitute the levels of your IV. Secondly, you may use the questionnaire/scale to *generate your DV*. For example, you may use an attitude scale to assess the impact of exposing subjects to different forms of a persuasive message. Thirdly, you may use your questionnaire/scale as a means of *splitting your subjects up into comparison groups* – e.g. into Extraverts and Introverts, those who are pro- and those who are anti-nuclear power, etc. Such groups are split on the basis of what are known as **classification variables**.

Studies that fall into the above categories should pose few problems for your DESIGN, at least once you've worked out what the IV's, DV's, or classification variables were, and whether your comparisons were between or within subjects. However, things are slightly more difficult when you use the questionnaire/scale more flexibly; when, for instance, you split your subjects up on the basis of their answers to particular questions at one time, and then use these same answers as the scores for other comparisons in the same study. For instance, you might use the answers to the question 'On average, how many cigarettes do you smoke a day?' as a means of splitting your subjects into light, moderate, and heavy smokers (i.e. as a *classifica-*

*tion variable*). However, in the same study you might use the answers to this same question as the scores for another comparison – e.g. in order to find out whether say, having parents who smoked (another classification variable) had any impact on the average number of cigarettes subjects smoked per day.

Strictly speaking, in such instances you have a number of *separate* designs, each one indicated by the particular comparisons you wish to make. The variables on which you split your subjects will probably be classification variables, the scores on which they are compared the equivalent of DVs. In order to write a proper DESIGN, therefore, you would need to work out what comparisons you made on which scores. The place to look for this information, of course, is the RESULTS.

Studies of all these types can be accommodated reasonably well within the traditional DESIGN section. The final use, however – the *survey* – is trickier. This is because such studies are *descriptive* (section 8.6) and therefore have no design in the strict experimental sense. Under these circumstances, you may well wish to replace the DESIGN, MATERIALS, and PROCEDURE with a section that describes the purposes of the survey, the development of the questionnaire, its final form, and means of administering it. Alternatively, you could probably report the above information reasonably in the traditional METHOD sections. But under these circumstances *don't* try to create some mythical design for your study involving IVs, DVs etc. This would be meaningless.

Finally, in all questionnaire/scale studies the balance between the MATERIALS and PROCEDURE tends to differ from that in more straightforward experimental studies. Where you have obtained the questionnaire/scale from the established literature, then you will need to cite the source of it in the MATERIALS, together with a brief account of its principal features (e.g. the format provided for the subjects' responses). Where, however, you have developed the questionnaire/scale yourself, your MATERIALS will probably be longer than usual, as you will need to include information on the structure of the questionnaire/scale, and how it was constructed. (In all cases put a copy of the questionnaire/scale itself in an appendix and discuss only the more critical features in the text.) Your PROCEDURE may be correspondingly shorter, as there may have been little procedural interaction between you and your subjects. But you should make sure that you provide the reader with an account of how the scale was administered, supervised, what you said to the subjects etc. That is, the sort of information necessary for someone to undertake an *exact replication* of your study.

# *Appendix 3  Randomizing*

This is an essential skill of the empirical psychologist – one that is consistently underrated by both teachers and students of the discipline. Indeed, the whole strength of the experiment as a tool for enabling us to make causal inferences in many ways depends on our ability to allocate subjects to conditions or conditions to subjects randomly. Fail to do this, and you lose one of the basic controls for confounding variables (section 9.5).

There are a number of occasions on which you will need to randomize. The first is when you need to randomize the order in which you present the conditions to your subjects. The second is the technique that is most generally employed to control for the effects of individual differences in a between subjects design. This is the random *allocation* of subjects to conditions. You may also need to use randomization when preparing your materials. Finally, if you go on to do research, you may eventually find yourself selecting subjects randomly from a hypothetical statistical population.

You will find advice on how to do most of these things below. It is important for you to realize however that the basic principle of randomization is the same in all these cases (although the method by which you realize this principle may differ). Thus, whatever you are randomizing – be it orders or subjects or words in a stimulus list – any given item should have an equal chance of selection *at all times* (i.e. the prior selection of one particular item should not affect in any way the chances of any of the other items being subsequently selected). So, for example, if you are selecting orders for your subjects, the chances of any given order being selected must not be affected by any selections that you have made previously. Similarly, when allocating subjects to conditions, the chances of a given subject appearing in one particular condition should not be affected by previous allocations to that or any other condition.

What this means in practice is that we don't simply sit down and juggle our orders around or allocate our subjects to conditions in what seems to us to be a suitably random order. Neither do we generate numbers from our heads. Such methods do *not* give us truly random results. Instead, we employ *tools*, devices that enable us to generate truly random sequences and whose results *we obey*, however non-random they appear.

Now, all that is required of these tools is that they make the choice for us in an unbiased way: i.e. that they do not favour some outcomes more than others. Consequently, if used properly, things like coins, playing cards, dice etc., are perfectly adequate for this purpose. In addition, most textbooks of statistics include tables of *random numbers*. These tables have been produced by a program that enabled the digits 0 to 9 to have an equal opportunity of appearing at any given position in the table. So, at any given position, you have no idea which of these digits is likely to appear. Even if the previous twelve digits have all been '7' (which is extremely unlikely, but still possible) the chances of '7' appearing as the thirteenth digit are *exactly the same* as if there had been no '7' among the previous twelve. You can see, therefore, that such tables are ideally suited for the purposes of randomizing.

You can use these digits singly, in pairs, groups of three and so on. The important thing is to make sure that you don't keep entering the tables at the same place. If you do, then you will simply be using the same sequence of numbers and your lists will not differ.

Finally, before we give you some examples of how you might go about randomizing in particular circumstances, it should be clear from section 3.5 that randomizing is one of the things that you should do, whenever possible, *prior* to running your subjects. That is, it is one of the elements of experimenting that you can usually organize *in advance*.

### Using the Tables

Enter the tables at a random position. Spin a coin to decide whether you will proceed diagonally (heads) or along lines (tails). If tails, spin a coin to decide whether you will move horizontally (heads) or vertically (tails). Then spin a coin to decide whether you will move up or down (if moving vertically) or left or right (if moving horizontally). Proceed similarly if the original spin had returned a head. This procedure is standard for the use of tables.

### Allocating Subjects to Groups

Suppose we wish to allocate 10 subjects to condition A and 10 to condition B.

Number your subjects 1 to 20, with numbers 1 to 10 in condition A, 11 to 20 in condition B. Enter the tables and proceed as directed above. Step through the tables reading *pairs* of digits. The order in which you come across these numbers will dictate the order in which you run your subjects. For instance, with the sequence:

23 53 04 01 63 08 45 93 15 22

your first three subjects will be from condition A (04, 01, and 08). Your fourth will be from condition B (15), and so on. Once a number has been encountered, however, you should disregard it on future occurrences (randomization *without* replacement).

This technique can obviously be extended to more than two conditions.

## Allocating Orders to Subjects

Even with a counterbalanced design you should allocate the orders to subjects randomly. For example, with our study in SAQ 38, we have six different orders. Suppose we wish to allocate these orders to twelve subjects.

Enter the tables and proceed as directed above. Number the subjects 1 to 12. Step through the tables looking for pairs of digits, allocating the subjects to the orders in sequence. For example, with the following line:

23 53 04 01 63 08 45 93 15 22

subject 4 would do order 1, subject 1 would do order 2, subject 8 order 3, and so on until all twelve subjects had received an order. Again, you should disregard repeats of particular numbers (randomization *without* replacement).

## Constructing Materials

Suppose you need to randomize the order in which a set of 30 questions appears in a questionnaire. Number the questions, and then step through the random number tables as directed above to obtain the order in which the questions should appear. For instance, with the sequence:

23 53 04 01 63 08 45 93 15 22

question 23 would come first, question 4 second, question 1 third, and so on.

You would probably need to produce more than one version of the questionnaire, so you would need to repeat the above process.

# Answers to SAQs

*SAQ 1*
(a) Results (b) Discussion.

*SAQ 2*
False. Even if this were true of the person who marks your report, it is certainly not true of the person for whom the report should be written – the hypothetical reader who is intelligent but unknowledgeable about your study and the area of psychology in which it took place.

*SAQ 3*
The INTRODUCTION, and the METHOD, because you will report in these sections material that you should have decided upon *prior* to undertaking the experiment.

*SAQ 4*
The DISCUSSION, because it is there that you will assess the implications of your findings. It is precisely for their implications that experiments are undertaken in the first place.

*SAQ 5*
You should attempt to *substantiate* it. The preferred method of doing this is by *referencing* previous work in the area. Where you are unable to find suitable references, you should use examples to justify your statement.

*SAQ 6*
The order of the references is not chronological. There are two references to Dawkins and Edgar (1977), neither of which are suffixed. Colons, rather than semi-colons, are used to separate the references. Abel, Baker, and Cartwright is repeated when the Latin '*et al.*,' could have been used. No page numbers are given for the quotation. The corrected references should read: (French, 1962, 1983; Dawkins and Edgar, 1977a, 1977b; Garbage, Henchman and Janitor, 1984).

*SAQ 7*
They are designed to facilitate the conveying of information about a study clearly, precisely, quickly, and concisely.

*SAQ 8*
In your INTRODUCTION you introduce your *study* to your *reader*. But remember that you must assume your reader is *psychologically naive* (Chapter 1). Which means that, as well as telling the reader all about the study you conducted, you must also put it into its context – that is, you must show how your study relates to previous work in the same area.

*SAQ 9*
Because your reader knows nothing about the area of psychology relevant to your study. In order to understand and evaluate your study, therefore, s/he has first to be told about previous relevant work in the area.

*SAQ 10*
Because the researcher will return in the DISCUSSION to the material summarized in the INTRODUCTION, and re-assess this material in the light of the study's *findings*. To the extent that these findings improve, illuminate, or qualify the picture presented in the INTRODUCTION, we have made progress.

*SAQ 11*
Because, as pointed out in Chapter 1, your report reflects the sequence in which you (theoretically) designed the experiment. The INTRODUCTION, therefore, should provide your reader with an outline of the reasoning that led to the design of your experiment in the first place. Consequently, it should describe the position you were in *prior* to running the experiment and, of course, could (in principle, rather than in practice) have been written at this stage – before the data was in.

*SAQ 12*
It serves to introduce your study to the reader. There are two aspects to this: firstly, an introduction to the area of psychology relevant to the study you conducted and, secondly, a brief description of your own study.

*SAQ 13*
An exact replication of a study occurs when the experiment is repeated in *exactly* the same way in order to examine the *reliability* of the findings obtained (i.e. to see if the same results are obtained). The whole point of the METHOD section is to provide the reader with sufficient information to enable him/her to undertake such a replication.

*SAQ 14*
Because, to all intents and purposes, the null hypothesis is the same for all experiments.

*SAQ 15*
The DESIGN serves to give the reader a brief, formal account of the precise design employed in your experiment. This information is essential for anyone who wishes to *replicate* your study.

*SAQ 16*
Because this would be a *confounding variable*. See Chapter 9 for information on how to avoid this problem.

*SAQ 17*
S/he needs to know (1) who they were and (2) how they were distributed across your experimental conditions. S/he needs to know (1) in order to assess the *generalizability* of your findings. S/he needs to know (2) in order to establish whether there are any *confounding variables* arising from the way in which the subjects were distributed across the various conditions.

*SAQ 18*
It is in the form of a list, when it should be in text. It has been labelled APPARATUS, when it contains both apparatus and materials. The precise makes and models of the equipment used are not given. Although a number of pieces of equipment have been used, we are given no idea of how they were linked together – a diagram would have been useful here.

Answers to SAQs

*SAQ 19*
If they weren't – if there *were* differences between your conditions other than those involving your manipulation of the IV – there would be a *confounding* variable in your experiment.

*SAQ 20*
Because if the instructions vary *between* conditions in aspects other than those involved in manipulating the IV, this would constitute a confounding variable. Similarly, if the instructions vary *within* conditions, this might not only increase the variability within that condition, but again, if uncontrolled, might constitute a confounding variable. Indeed, there is evidence to suggest that subjects' behaviour can be strongly influenced by even quite subtle changes in instructions. So if we want to be able to make any sense of the results we obtain, we need to keep our instructions as constant as we can within any given study.

*SAQ 21*
Your reader needs to be able to satisfy him/herself that the data you gathered was appropriate to the question you claim to be examining, that the inferential statistics you calculated were appropriate given your data, and that the outcomes of these analyses appear to be consistent with the data as described by your descriptive statistics. S/he needs this information in order to evaluate your findings.

*SAQ 22*
Firstly, we are given no indication as to which data is being analysed. Secondly, the description of the analysis is imprecise. Thirdly, we are given no details of the precise outcomes of the analysis, the degrees of freedom, nor the significance level employed. Finally, we have no idea what these results mean in real terms. A more appropriate statement would run as follows: 'The data in Table 1 were analysed using a 1-way, between subjects analysis of variance. There was a significant effect of presentation rate upon recall ($F2,15 = 7.45$; $p<0.05$).'

*SAQ 23*
Because (1) confounding variables represent alternative explanations for our findings, and (2) controlled variables – ones whose values are held *constant* throughout the experiment – may represent limitations on the *generalizability* of our findings.

*SAQ 24*
No. It may be that at other temperatures – for instance, chilled – they *could* taste the difference. Indeed, temperature appears to markedly affect the flavour of a drink, as any beer or wine drinker can tell you. In order to test this possibility, of course, we would need to *manipulate* the temperature variable, rather than hold it constant. So our findings may only hold for the conditions employed in the experiment. And whether people *in general* are unable to taste the difference, of course, depends also on how representative a group of OU students at this summer school are of the population at large.

*SAQ 25*
The purpose of the DISCUSSION is to enable you to assess the implications of your findings for the area of psychology relevant to the study you undertook. It is, therefore, the key section of the report, for it is at this stage that we are able to discover how much progress our findings have enabled us to make.

*SAQ 26*
They serve to alert potential readers to the existence of an article that may be of interest to them.

*SAQ 27*
The variable we manipulate is called the *Independent Variable* (IV). The variable we measure is called the *Dependent Variable* (DV).

a. The IV is the frequency of the words (High, Medium, and Low). The DV is the subjects' reaction time in milliseconds.
b. The IV is whether the rat had been injected with oestrogen or saline.
The DV is the body weight of the rats in grammes.
c. The IV is the level of anxiety induced by the programme (high, moderate, and, low).
The DV is the number of those in each group who take up the opportunity to make a dental appointment.
d. The IV is the nature of the violence depicted in the programme (realistic, unrealistic, or, none).
The DV is the mean level of shock the viewers subsequently give their victims in volts.
e. The IV is whether the subjects were working alone, or with one, two, four, or, eight, co-workers.
The DV is the number of cereal packets put into boxes during the 20 minute period.

*SAQ 28*
The *independent* variable is whether or not the subject consumed the standard quantity of cheese three hours before going to bed. The *dependent* variable is the number of nightmares reported by the two groups.
What we have done here, in essence, is play around with the amount of cheese eaten by the members of the two groups, and looked to see if this has any effect on the incidence of nightmares. Thus cheese eating is the suspected cause and nightmares the measured effect.

*SAQ 29*
The control condition in our cheese and nightmare experiment is the one in which *no* cheese is given to the subjects.

*SAQ 30*
There are five conditions in this experiment, four of which are *experimental* conditions (Cheddar, Caerphilly, Red Leicester, and Cheshire) and one *control* condition (no cheese).

*SAQ 31*
a. 3 (high, medium, low word frequency)
b. 2 (oestrogen, saline injections)
c. 3 (high, moderate, low anxiety arousal)
d. 3 (realistic, unrealistic, no violence)
e. 5 (alone, 1, 2, 4, 8 co-workers)
Experiments b (saline), d (no violence), and e (alone) have *control* conditions.

*SAQ 32*
No. There are in fact two other possible outcomes. This particular piece of folk wisdom might, for example, be the wrong way around. That is, instead of giving you

149

nightmares, eating cheese might actually enhance sleep and suppress nightmares. In which case we might expect those in the no-cheese condition to actually report a *higher* frequency of nightmares than those in the cheese condition. On the other hand, it may be that cheese has no effect whatsoever upon the incidence of nightmares. In which case we would expect to find little or no difference in the number of nightmares reported by the two groups of subjects.

*SAQ 33*
a. The reaction time of the subjects will not be the same for the high, medium, and low frequency words.
b. The changes in body weight will not be the same among those rats injected with oestrogen as among those rats injected with saline.
c. The number of viewers making dental appointments will not be the same among those who watched the high, moderate, and low anxiety-arousing programmes.
d. The mean level of shock administered by the subjects to the victim will not be the same after viewing programmes which depict realistic, unrealistic and no violence.
e. The number of packets of breakfast cereal packed by the workers will not be the same when they work alone, or with 1, 2, 4, and 8, co-workers.

*SAQ 34*
The uni-directional hypothesis. For, in stating which of our conditions will exceed the other on the DV, (e.g. that the subjects in our cheese condition will experience *more* nightmares than those in the control condition) we are of course stating the *direction* of the difference between them. If we are only prepared to state that there will be a difference of some sort between our conditions, but not to say anything about the direction of this difference (i.e. if we make a bi-directional experimental hypothesis) then our experimental hypothesis is of course *non-directional*.

*SAQ 35*
No. This relationship probably occurs because of a third *causal* variable – ambient temperature. That is, as the temperature rises, so more ice-cream is consumed and, quite independently, so more people go swimming. And, as more people swim, so more people die in drowning accidents. So any apparently causal link between these variables is entirely spurious.

*SAQ 36*
Our original cheese and nightmare experiment had different subjects in our two conditions. Hence it had a *between* subjects design. We could also have run it by comparing the number of nightmares reported by the same subjects on nights in which they had eaten cheese with the number reported on nights in which they hadn't eaten cheese. This would have been a *within* subjects design.

*SAQ 37*
a. Within subjects
b. Between subjects
c. Between subjects
d. Between subjects
e. Within subjects

*SAQ 38*
a. As we have three conditions, there are only six different ways in which we can order these conditions. Thus, it is quite feasible to *counterbalance* them. The orders are:

Hi   Med  Lo
Hi   Lo   Med
Med  Hi   Lo
Med  Lo   Hi
Lo   Med  Hi
Lo   Hi   Med

As you can see, therefore, each condition appears an equal number of times in each position, and an equal number of times before and after each other condition – i.e. the experiment is fully counterbalanced.

As we have six different orders, then we need a minimum of six subjects for our experiment. Of course we would use more than this. But of course our total number of subjects would have to be divisible by six.

b. We have five conditions. There are, therefore, 120 different ways of ordering these conditions (five factorial = $5 \times 4 \times 3 \times 2 \times 1 = 120$). We would therefore require a minimum of 120 subjects to fully counterbalance this experiment. Consequently, we would probably be better off *randomizing*. We would do this by allocating one of the 120 possible orders randomly to each of our subjects. This method of controlling for order effects does not limit the number of subjects we can employ, so there is no minimum. However, the more we employ, the more effective will be our randomizing, and – other things being equal – the more reliable our data.

## SAQ 39
Otherwise there is the possibility of a *confounding* variable arising from the non-random allocation of subjects to conditions, just as with non-matched subjects.

## SAQ 40
1. The factors are: level of alcohol, sex, and driving experience (time since passing driving test). Hence there are three factors. The first of these is a within subjects factor, the other two are necessarily between subjects factors. Thus it is a mixed design. The answer, therefore, is a three-factor, mixed design.
b. The factors are: type of stress, and nature of task. Hence there are two factors. The first is a between subjects factor, the second a within subjects factor. Thus it is a mixed design. The answer, therefore, is a two-factor, mixed design.
c. The factors are: sex, and Extraversion. Hence there are two factors. These are both necessarily between subjects factors. Thus it is a between subjects design. The answer, therefore, is a two-factor, between subjects design.
d. The factors are: driving conditions, nature of listening material, and volume level. Hence there are three factors. All of these are within subjects factors. Thus it is a within subjects design. The answer, therefore, is a three-factor, within subjects design.

Note that it is the number of *factors* (IV's) that is important, not the number of levels (conditions) on these factors. You have been able to correctly label the above designs without any knowledge of the number of levels the experimenters used on each factor.

## SAQ 41
One. Given by $(2-1) \times (2-1) = 1 \times 1 = 1$. Those of you who are confused by this concept please note that you have been able to calculate the appropriate figure *without* having to know what it actually refers to.

## SAQ 42
A value of p=0.05 is nearer zero than one. It is, therefore, nearer the impossible end of the continuum. Thus it is an event that is *unlikely* to occur by chance. But note that

151

it does not have a probability of zero. Thus it is still *possible* for it to occur by chance. Hence, our event is *possible but unlikely*. And (sigh!) that's the rub.

*SAQ 43*
Yes. The probability associated with our obtained version of chi-square is less than p=0.05. It is therefore significant at the five per cent significance level.

*SAQ 44*
1. We wish to compare conditions, so we need a test of differences. The data – reaction times in milliseconds – are interval. We wish to compare 3 conditions, on 1 IV, and we have obtained our scores from the same subjects. The major candidates are a *1-way, within subjects Analysis of Variance*, if we consider that our data satisfies the requirements of *parametric* tests, or the *Friedman* test if we don't.
2. We wish to compare conditions, so we need a test of differences. The data – body weights in grammes – are *interval*. We wish to compare 2 conditions, on 1 IV, and we have obtained our scores from *different* subjects. The major candidates are the *1-way, between subjects Analysis of Variance* or the *independent t-test* if we consider that our data satisfies the requirements of *parametric* tests, or the *Mann-Whitney U test*, if we don't.
3. The data – the number of subjects who make dental appointments – are *nominal*. We wish to compare 3 conditions, on 1 IV, and we have obtained our scores from *different* subjects. The main candidate is *chi-square*.
4. We wish to compare conditions, so we need a test of differences. The data – mean level of shock in volts – are *interval*. We wish to compare 3 conditions, on 1 IV, and our scores were obtained from *different* subjects. The main candidates are the *1-way, between subjects Analysis of Variance*, if we consider that our data satisfies the requirements of *parametric* tests, or the *Kruskal–Wallis test* if we don't.
5. We wish to compare conditions, so we need a test of differences. The data – the number of packets of cereal – are *interval*. We wish to compare 5 conditions, on 1 IV, and our scores were obtained from the *same* subjects. The main candidates are the *1-way, within subjects Analysis of Variance*, if we consider that our data satisfies the requirements of *parametric* tests, or the *Friedman test*, if we don't.

*SAQ 45*
The probability for a two-tailed test is twice that for the one-tailed version. The probability associated with t=6.31 with one degree of freedom, two-tailed, is therefore p=0.1, or ten per cent.

*SAQ 46*
1. The critical value of W for N=22 at the 5 per cent level (2-tailed) is W=66. As our obtained W is *less* than this, our result is significant.
2. The critical value of U for n1=10, n2=12 at the 5 per cent level (2-tailed) is U=29. As our obtained value of U is *less* than this, our result is significant.
3. The critical value of $\chi^2$ with 1df at the 5 per cent level (2-tailed) is $\chi^2$=3.84. As our obtained value of 2 is *less* than this, our result is *not* significant.
4. The critical value of t with 16 df's at the 5 per cent level (2-tailed) is t=2.12. As our obtained value of $\chi^2$ is *less* than this, our result is *not* significant.
5. The critical value of F with df1=2 and df2=25 at the 5 per cent level (2-tailed) is F=3.39. As our obtained value of F is *greater* than this, our result is significant.

Note that whether your *obtained* value has to exceed or be less than the critical value depends on the statistic in question (Table 4.3). There are sound statistical reasons for this.

*SAQ 47*

If you *reject* the null hypothesis. This means that you have found evidence enough to persuade you that there is a difference between your conditions on the DV. So this is evidence *against* the proposition that predicted that there would be no difference. Thus, in this sort of experiment you can only ever find evidence that goes against propositions that predict no difference, not evidence in favour of them.

# *Index*

Index of Concepts